TORTURE MOM

A CHILLING TRUE STORY OF CONFINEMENT, MUTILATION AND MURDER

RYAN GREEN

Disclaimer

This book is about real people committing real crimes. The story has been constructed by facts but some of the scenes, dialogue and characters have been fictionalised.

Polite Note to the Reader

This book is written in British English except where fidelity to other languages or accents are appropriate. Some words and phrases may differ from US English.

For Helen, Harvey, Frankie and Dougie

CONTENTS

Introduction

Jenny lay on the heap of dirty clothes that was meant to be her bed and stared up at the blue smoke curling across the ceiling. Here in the bedroom, it wasn't too suffocating but if she crawled out into the hallway then it was as thick as fog. The smoke wasn't keeping her awake. She had gotten used to the smoke in this house—she had accepted that it was going to stain anything white to yellow and make her clothes, her hair and even her skin reek like an ashtray.

From down the hallway, she could hear the chatter of voices and the warbling of one of Stephanie's records. There was never a moment when the kids from the neighbourhood weren't lingering around the house, smoking and sharing their snide little secrets. There wasn't enough money for food, but they always had cigarettes: the visitors, the children of the house and 'Mother'. Jenny strained to listen for the old woman's voice underneath all the hubbub. It was shrill and nasal. It would cut through what the children were saying with ease. Jenny couldn't hear it.

There were no doors in the house. Privacy was an invitation to sin. The old woman stalked around whenever she could be bothered to move, peering into every dark corner to make sure that none of the girls were straying from purity. If she had been speaking, then Jenny was sure that she would hear it. But if the old woman wasn't spitting poison through there, then it meant that she could be standing over Jenny right at that moment.

Looking back on them now, the beatings hadn't been too bad. The violence and the cruelty had been the worst that Jenny had ever experienced in her life—the welts that had been left across the backs of her legs had burned and stung every time that she moved—but compared to the evil that she now knew was lurking just under the surface in every single person she met, Jenny understood that a few whacks with a stick was far from the worst thing to happen to a person. She closed her eyes and tried to look like she was asleep. Maybe the old woman would just pass her by if she came in and Jenny was sleeping.

The nasal whine raised hairs on the back of her neck when Jenny finally picked it out, a high-pitched wheeze that she was pretty sure only dogs should have been able to hear. It was the old woman's snoring. She must have fallen asleep in her chair.

Jenny's eyes popped open and she gasped with relief. The danger wasn't completely past: any one of the monsters in the other room could still torture her at the drop of a hat, but there were limits to how much they would be willing to do without permission. The old woman may have just seemed like a skeleton stuffed in a skin suit, but with a look or a word, she could bring any one of the children to their knees. Nothing happened without her permission, whether it was explicit, or implied.

For a little while, Jenny just lay there, feeling the fear start to ebb out of her body. She had never really known fear before she came to this house, not the bone-deep dread that followed her everywhere that she went now. Knowing the specifics of what could and probably would happen to her was worse than anything that her imagination could have manufactured. She would not have been able to imagine what burning human flesh smelled like before tonight, and a year ago she would not have been able to imagine being so hungry that it would smell appetising. The fear had burrowed so deeply into her heart that it had changed her in ways that were so insidious she hadn't even noticed to begin with.

It started innocently enough, one of the girls would make a mean comment and Jenny would laugh along even though it wasn't funny because it was easier to fit in than to stand out. Going against any of them came with dangers, but while the boys might shove her or kick her crutches away, the girls went whispering back to the old woman. Jenny barely ate as it was. She couldn't afford to lose any more meals. The real proof of how far she had fallen was when the social worker came. She repeated every vile lie that the old woman had hissed into her ear without flinching. Just the hint of a threat was enough to leave her numb and quaking for days. Just the simple words, 'Do you want to go to the basement?'

When Jenny started to cry she was careful to muffle it with her sleeve. It wouldn't be good for one of the children to hear her. It would be even worse if the old woman was disturbed. Jenny would do anything to avoid the awful weight of that woman's attention. The children weren't safe by any stretch of the imagination. Jenny pictured them as hyenas wearing human clothes most of the time, braying and just waiting for the opportunity to tear into her flesh the moment that she seemed defenceless. But the old woman held their leash, and as long as she didn't decide to set them on Jenny, she would be safe. She kept telling herself that she would be safe soon. As if this nightmare had an expiry date already decided. In a way, it did. The thing in the basement would determine how much more of this misery Jenny had to endure before all of this family's dark intent was focused exclusively on her. She struggled to get her breathing under control, to turn her gasps and sobs into the quiet breathing of a girl asleep. The old woman might not be able to see her, but a sniffle at the wrong moment could unravel all of her hard work pretending to be one of the pack.

If she thought about the basement for too long, Jenny started to feel sick. She couldn't afford to lose her appetite any more than she could afford to lose a meal as punishment. She could feel her bones pressing up under her skin when she ran her hands over herself. Not that she dared to even touch herself over her clothes anymore. Not after the lecture on sin and self-pollution that the old woman had inflicted on them after the last time she caught one of the boys adjusting himself.

When she was afraid, Jenny didn't even dare to think about the basement—far too keenly aware that she might end up there. But in these brief moments when the tide of dread was out, she refused to think about it, more often than not, because thinking about it hurt, and she was hurting too much these days. When polio had ravaged her, she knew that there were going to be aches and pains for the rest of her life, but she couldn't recall them ever being so intense as when she had come to this house. She was beaten very rarely, even compared to the old woman's own children, but with nothing to eat, she sometimes thought that her body was quietly consuming itself.

This night was different. The sharp pangs of terror that the basement usually brought on had been drowned out with anticipation. Tension had been thrumming in the air ever since the gruesome display earlier on. Even if it had gone back down to a simmer now, it was soon going to boil over. She told herself that everything was going to be okay. She told herself that she didn't really believe time was running out. That the thing in the basement was still going to be there for years to come. Tears started to prick at the corners of her eyes again. Everything was going to be fine. Nothing was going to go wrong. Everything was going to be fine. Jenny had always been a terrible liar.

She pulled herself up to sitting and strained to hear any hint of movement from the other room. The laughter had turned raucous, the old woman was snoring steadily, there was never going to be a safer time for her to move. There was never going to be another chance to take this risk. Her crutches were propped in the corner, and they made such a racket that there was no possibility of sneaking around if she used them, so instead Jenny dragged herself slowly across the dust-caked floor to peer out into the hall. Through the blue fog, she could see the silhouettes in the living room. The shadows in the shape of people that she could have mistaken for human beings if she didn't remember what she had seen that day. The old woman was out of sight, but the trilling of her snores was unmistakable. Jenny could do this. Everything was going to be fine.

She dragged herself along the hallway, letting her weak legs take only a portion of her weight in case she needed them rested for a mad rush back to bed if there were any sign of trouble. It took longer than it should have to travel down the short hall, swerving to avoid mounds of trash or heaps of empty cola bottles. She made it to the kitchen unnoticed, but when the door to the basement stood before her, she froze.

It had been a long time since she had last willingly gone down those stairs, and back then the possibility of being locked down there in the basement hadn't even occurred to Jenny. She could already smell the thing down in the basement. Even from up here with the door closed the stench of it wafted up. The sickly sweetness of ammonia undercutting the farmyard stench of excrement. Jenny started breathing through her mouth. She could do this. Everything was going to be fine. The door creaked as she pressed it open and it was all that she could do to keep herself from scrambling back to bed. For another dreadful moment, she held herself still, kneeling on the kitchen floor and feeling the weight of it all pressing down on her. She strained for any sign from the living room that she had been heard, but after a moment another ripple of laughter assured her that she had gone unnoticed. With a brush of her fingertips, the door swung open the rest of the way and Jenny looked down into the abyss.

Beyond the reach of the light from the bare bulb hanging in the kitchen was a darkness so complete that Jenny could barely understand it. As if the stairs led down to a solid black wall with nothing beyond that point. All of the fear that she had quashed came rushing back. How could anyone live in that total darkness? How could you open your eyes to nothingness when you woke up and close your eyes on it when you tried to fall asleep? She stared into that darkness and tried to will her body forward. She was vulnerable kneeling out here in the open. If she went down the stairs, then she would be safer. That lie was so big that she couldn't even get through telling it to herself before rejecting it. Just as she was about to turn tail and flee back to bed, she heard a sound from beneath her.

Down in the basement, the thing had heard her coming. Jenny could hear it even now, scratching around on the packed dirt of the floor. It knew that she was here. Somehow it knew. She heard something like a sob echoing up from the darkness, and that was enough to strengthen her resolve. She crab-walked down the stairs, lowering herself carefully to stay silent and not even flinching when she pushed the door shut behind her, blocking out the last of the light. In that deep darkness, she felt her way forward, step by step, muscles aching from the effort, heart hammering in her chest. This could be her life. If she was caught coming down here, this would be her life.

She almost ran again when her foot brushed against dirt instead of another step, but instead, she forced herself upright. Down here in the hot darkness the smell was almost overpowering. Every breath was a struggle not to gag. It was like stepping inside a septic tank. She staggered forward a couple of steps before her foot brushed against something unmistakable. Bare human flesh. With quaking hands, Jenny bent down and touched her sister's arm. Following the emaciated lines of it down to where her hand was curled into a claw. She wasn't sure when she had started crying, but now it wouldn't stop. A whisper croaked out of the darkness. 'Jenny?'

'I'm here. I'm here now. Everything is going to be okay.'

Sylvia's breath came out like a rattle, but there was no fear in her voice when she answered.

'I'm going to die.'

Gertrude Van Fossan

In the late September of 1929, America was about to plummet from a precipice. In less than a month the Wall Street Stock Exchange would crash, plunging the country into the Great Depression. The working class of America would struggle and die by the thousands as the intermittently prosperous nation experienced its worst economic collapse in history. Homes would be repossessed, businesses would collapse and the boom following World War I that many had hoped would continue forever would instead drag the whole nation to the verge of collapse.

At this time of great upheaval and impending doom, a baby girl was born. Gertrude Van Fossan was the third of an eventual six children in the Van Fossan family. The Van Fossans were of mixed ancestry, combining a long line of Polish immigrants on her mother's side with a better established Dutch family on the other. Very little is known about the early years of her life, except that she was quite firmly a daddy's girl, spending every moment that she could with her father, who doted on her. In tough times, attention was the only currency that the Van Fossan family really had to spend, so it was unsurprising that the other members of the family soon came to resent how close that relationship had become. The elder children tolerated it well because the youngest was always going to be the centre of parental attention, but even after new babies were born into the family, Gert still got the lion's share of affection.

Her mother perceived the closeness of the relationship as a threat when her daughter was only a toddler and did all that she could to separate her from her father, but it did no good. Swiftly, this 'concern' transformed into a coldness that bordered on hatred. When her father was out of the house, Gert lived in a frosty silence, with her mother barking instructions but otherwise ignoring her entirely. Viewed in contrast to the relationships that her mother had with the other children, this only made her poor treatment more pronounced. The other five children in the house behaved exactly as one would expect. They saw Gert as different—an outsider—and they isolated her.

This only exacerbated the problem. With only one source of affection in her life, Gert clung to her father ever more desperately. While he did not understand the situation that he was abandoning her to when he left the house, he did recognise that desperation and he responded as any kind and loving father would: by lavishing even more attention on her than his other children. It took very little work for Gert's mother to turn the other children against her completely, and even when she attended school she was bullied, both by friends of the other Van Fossan children and others who merely preyed on the isolated girl. Her schooling was inconsistent in those early years, partly because of the complete lack of interest from her mother in ensuring that she attended, but also because Gert chose to avoid situations where she would be at a disadvantage.

The family did not weather the Great Depression well, nor did their hometown of Indianapolis. Gert's father went through several jobs and took to drinking when he could afford it. Her mother blamed Gert for all of her father's failings and most of the other troubles that befell the family, but as Gert was her father's favourite there was nothing that could be said or done against her without reprisals. While she wasn't having a healthy and happy childhood, her father saw to it that Gert wasn't entirely devoid of joy, and just the mention of him was enough to bring a smile to her face. As long as he was around, she had hope for a better future.

Daddy had been home for a couple of hours and dinner was over. It had been another 'tight' week, so dinner hadn't been much more than soup and Daddy hadn't had a thing to drink. Instead, he had shooed mother and the other children out of the kitchen and was now sitting there in his chair by the oven listening to Gert practicing her reading. She didn't read well, and she knew it. She wasn't stupid just because she was ten. But for Daddy she was willing to put in the effort, to struggle through each tangle of letters and get it right, because when she did she could see that smile creeping over his face. It made her feel warm even when the wind was howling and the windows popped out of their frames a little. When she got to the end of the page he actually clapped his hands together and it was all that she could do to resist bouncing up and down on the spot. That smile. She would remember that smile every day for the rest of her life. Daddy made some joke about the already forgotten page that she had just read and she laughed along just like she was meant to. She could tell it was a joke by the little crinkles by his eyes; they were a dead giveaway every time he was being funny with her. When she laughed, he laughed along with her, so in about a second they were both laughing about nothing and it was the best part of Gert's day. In the other room she could hear mother snapping at the little ones, outside she could hear the wind whipping by, but here in this kitchen, everything was warm and perfect. When Daddy made a silly face, her giggles got even more pronounced. The crinkles disappeared from beside his eyes, but that silly face kept her laughing. It was as if he had seen a ghost. His eyes were bulging like they would pop out of his head. She kept laughing as he toppled forward off his chair. His face bounced off the corner of the table on his way to the floor. Her fit of giggles turned into a strangled shriek. 'Daddy?!'

She scrambled down onto the floor beside him. Blood was oozing lazily from his forehead and pooling underneath him, but his eyes were still bulging wide open. 'Daddy!' He jerked and bucked on the floor like he was wrestling with some unseen force. Whatever he was trying to throw off was overpowering him easily. He let out a groan so deep that it barely sounded human. Gert had her hands full of his shirt and she was screaming. 'Daddy. Stop it! Daddy!'

Mother came barrelling into the room and let out a matching wail when she saw her husband lying there. She shoved Gert aside and started bellowing his name. Shaking him. She reared up and slapped him in the face, still screaming. The other children peered in through the door, curiosity and horror vying for a place on their vacant little faces. Gert tried to get back to her father, but her mother stopped her with a jab of her finger. She hissed, 'What did you do to him?!'

Gert couldn't get a breath in between her sobs. 'He was... He was laughing. Then he just fell. He just fell over!'

Mother's eyes narrowed. 'Get out.'

Gert scrambled back, eyes darting between Daddy and the woman hanging over him like a vulture. She couldn't do as she was told. It was like there was an elastic cord stretching from her heart to her daddy and every step away from him put more strain on it. 'Should... Should I get the doctor?'

Mother's voice cracked. 'Do you have doctor money? I don't.'

One of the other children cried from the doorway. 'What should we do, mommy?'

In an instant, their mother sprang into action, gathering up the children and shooing them away from the door. All the kindness that she denied Gert rolled off her in waves, calming the other children. Gert slipped back into her place by her father's side. In the other room, her mother was telling the children some lie about Daddy going to heaven. He wasn't going anywhere. He was right here on the kitchen floor. She burrowed into him, letting the ebbing warmth of his body surround her and straining to hear the beating of his heart. She didn't hear a thing.

If Gert had hoped that her relationship with her mother was going to improve with the death of her father, she was sorely mistaken. In addition to being irrationally blamed for her father's death, she reacted badly to the trauma of the event itself. She began to experience night terrors and without her father to act as counterbalance, her mother's cruelty escalated again and she began to beat Gert for disturbing the sleep of the other children.

The next three years were a living hell for Gert. She was treated worse than an animal at home, completely ignored by her mother and carefully ostracised by her siblings to avoid any taint from associating with her. In the mythology of the household, she was the root of all evil. Whenever something was wrong with a household item, Gert had been the last to use it. Whenever there wasn't enough food to go around, it was because Gert had taken more than her fair share. It got to the point of a running joke that the other children would bark out Gert's name whenever they so much as stubbed their toe.

In school, her social life remained desolate for another three years, but then something amazing happened. By the age of fourteen, Gert had abandoned all hope of female friendship. Her mother had poisoned that well early on in her life, and the constant spreading of rumours by the girls in her class regarding Gert's status as a pariah had left her soured to the very idea of spending time with other women. Boys were her only real option, but she didn't dare to defy her mother enough to be considered a tomboy, and without some common ground she just wasn't interesting to the preteens. The sudden onset of puberty and the associated rush of hormones changed all of that. Suddenly boys were interested in Gert again and she revelled in all of the attention. Her mother heard rumours early on and screeched at her daughter for the impropriety of her behaviour, but up until that point, Gert wasn't even aware that anything 'wrong' was going on.

She was aware of sex in an abstract way. When her father had been alive she would often hear unusual sounds coming from her parents' bedroom and was always dismayed the next morning to discover that her father would take sides with her mother in any ongoing arguments. She could not connect those sounds and the very gentle flirting that she was experiencing with the boys at school. She did not understand why her mother was so furious at her, but she was past the point of caring. Any punishment that could be inflicted on Gert already had been. There was nothing more that her mother could do to make her life miserable. Drawn by the promise of the attention that she had been so desperately craving, it was no wonder that Gert made the choices that she did.

The other girls may have been shyer to start with, but soon Gert was in competition with every single one of them for the affection and attention of the boys in school. Gert could charitably be described as average looking, and her personality had never had the opportunity to flourish with no social outlet. She began to push past her own boundaries of comfort and decency to keep the boys' attention. She would let them touch her in places that she knew she shouldn't. She would touch them back. The rumour mill went into overdrive, spreading malicious whispers about her antics around the whole town and it was widely considered to be just a matter of time before she got knocked up. For the first time, Gert felt like the whisper network of girls was actually helping her. Every boy in the school was suddenly interested in her, and plenty of boys who she had never even heard of started to come calling for her, too.

To her mother's absolute horror, Gert began dating in earnest by the time that she was fifteen, moving on from the little kisses and fumbles that she had dealt out to her schoolboy friends to the pursuit of real relationships. In her entire life up until that point, Gert had had only one successful relationship, the one with her father, so it was hardly surprising that she was drawn to older men. She was courted by a succession of men between two and eight years her senior, almost all of them pursuing her because of the sordid reputation that she had developed about the town. At the age of sixteen, she finally escaped from her horrible home life through the only mechanism that was available to women at that time. She dropped out of school, packed up the few meagre possessions that could be considered hers and left her mother's shadow, never to return.

Gertrude Baniszewski

Gert married John Baniszewski only a few months after they had begun dating. He was an eighteen-year-old police deputy with a good career ahead of him. The wedding was a fairly subdued affair, with only John's family in attendance. Gert didn't have any friends of her own, her mother loudly disapproved of her relationship with John to anyone who would listen, and she had no intention of involving any of her siblings in her life from that day forward. It was as if Gert's mother's wish had finally come true: her daughter vanished.

Even though John wasn't earning much, the local bank was happy to help out an officer of the law, and the two of them settled into a modest house on the edge of suburbia immediately after their brief honeymoon in Ohio. John had little control over his work schedule in those early days, so the young lovers took whatever time that they could get together, with Gert often popping down to the station to deliver a bagged lunch around the middle of John's shift. Sandwiches were pretty much the only thing that Gert knew how to prepare at that point in her life. Her mother had thrust many chores on her but never trusted her in the kitchen, and almost immediately her atrocious cooking put a strain on the new relationship. John had been drawn in by rumours about Gert's sexual expertise, but after spending some time with her he had realised that she would fulfil the role of wife perfectly well. She wasn't just content with the idea of playing house and raising children for the rest of her days; she was also sharp enough that he felt like he could trust her to handle the running of his household. As was often the case with young men living alone, he felt the need not only for companionship and romance but also for a replacement for his mother.

He had assumed that he was going to get a submissive and obedient servant out of the deal, but he was sorely mistaken. Gert kept the house as tidy as she could manage, nagging at John for making a mess when he was at home. She was frugal with the household budget, often chastising John for his spending too much when he went out drinking with his buddies after work. All of her virtues soon turned into vices. John had expected her cooking to improve with time, but by the end of their first year together she still wasn't capable of doing much more than John himself could. Worse still, the one area of marital life where John had expected her to excel—

in the bedroom—was where she disappointed him even worse than everywhere else. To Gert, sex was a mortal sin; it was a painful, distasteful chore that she had to endure to pay for this life that she had so desperately wanted. While her clumsy fumblings had been more than enough to satisfy boys her own age, John had some experience with women and he felt like he had been defrauded. When it became clear that she had no idea what she was doing he let his disappointment show, and that only led to her becoming even more withdrawn and distant. The problem escalated, with Gert becoming almost catatonic during their lovemaking and John becoming ever more violent until eventually, that violence bore fruit.

Over the course of the first decade of their marriage, Gert was pregnant more often than not, and they eventually had four children. Gert's entire personality shifted once she became pregnant for the first time. Every part of the home had to be spotless, well beyond her usual slack standards, after she had learned about the risks of infection to her unborn child. Her cooking finally began to improve as she heard from doctors about the importance of nutrition and began to pick up hints and tips from the other young mothers who attended clinics. She never formed friendships with any of these women, but she had finally come to recognise that other people were a resource that she could exploit.

Initially, John was pleased with the change that had come over Gert. Even if she wouldn't willingly let him touch her—

'to protect the baby'—she was finally growing into the wife that he had always expected her to be. Once the baby was born, that contentment turned back into frustration. Where before she had been obsessively attentive to John's needs, she had now found a new centre for her life. She could not make John into a man like her father. She would never have the close, intense relationship that she so desperately craved with him, so she had switched her focus to her children: tiny little people who she could mould into the perfect partners to accompany her through life. Everything that she couldn't be bothered to do for John, she did for the children willingly. Every moment of her time was devoted to them, and the same jealousy that had blighted Gert's childhood home soon started to rear its ugly head again.

It isn't clear exactly when John started to beat Gert. It didn't happen during any of her pregnancies or immediately after she had given birth, but the rest of the time seemed to be open season. The reason given for the sometimes-brutal bouts of domestic violence was that Gert was annoying him. She made no attempt to escape from the situation at the time, believing that it was just another unpleasant experience that she had to endure to have the life that she wanted. Sometimes the annoyance was that she was making too much noise. Other times it was simply that he didn't like the way that she looked at him. She was never hospitalised by the beatings, although on several occasions she probably should have been. John realised that going too far might damage his standing in the community and jeopardise his job, so he was careful in his abuse—using Gert as a punching bag but making sure not to lose control. He had years of experience dealing with beaten wives by that point in his career and he knew what triggered investigations. He was well liked around the station, so even if she had made a report it would have gotten lost, but he preferred to be careful.

During that decade, Gert suffered repeated injuries to the head, sometimes leaving her dizzy and disoriented for days afterwards and sometimes leaving her too bruised to venture out to the minimarket to buy food for the week. She got better at cooking, more inventive, able to stretch leftovers out over an extra day when she needed to. She got better with her makeup, too. Her mother had never taught her how to put it on. Such a thing would have been shameful on a little girl — whorish—but Gert learned by watching other women in public bathrooms. The first time she saw someone powdering on foundation it was like a revelation, and suddenly the waiting time between a beating and venturing outside again was halved.

The revelation of foundation was nothing compared to the day that Gert learned about divorce. It had always been a topic only spoken of in hushed tones when she was growing up. As a child, she had known that it was something so wrong that they weren't supposed to speak about it, but not what it actually entailed. By the time she had four children she wasn't quite that naïve anymore, but it was still an abstract concept, a punishment for truly terrible wives who didn't submit to their husband's whims. It was only when she caught a whisper of the local gossip about a woman in her own neighbourhood divorcing her husband that she truly realised that it was a possibility. She was almost overwhelmed by the idea. The word 'divorce' hung heavy in her head all through the rest of the week. The next time that she annoyed John, he lifted a hand to smack her and it slipped out from between her lips like a mantra. He had frozen, fist clenched, eyes bulging, and in that moment she realised just how impotent he had become. By the next week, she had the paperwork filed and the courts had awarded her full custody of the children. John didn't even try to contest it.

Gertrude Guthrie

It was only a few short months later that Gert found herself a new husband in Edward Guthrie. Gert's second wedding somehow managed to provide even less of a pleasant experience for her than the first, with the entire Guthrie clan of Indianapolis in attendance and drinking heavily throughout the night.

She was still young, and as pretty as she had ever been, and Eddie seemed charming compared to her brute of an ex-husband. He was unemployed when he met Gert and it was quite possible that a big part of her appeal was that she came with child support payments attached. While John had been a social drinker, wasting his paycheques down at the bar with the other policemen, Eddie was more serious in his pursuit of oblivion. He would pilfer each cheque as it came through the door and spend at least half of it on liquor before Gert even knew that it existed. They weren't drastically worse off than when she was married to John. The children still got fed, clothed and sent off to school. She still doted on them like only a mother would. They wanted for nothing, and if Gert had to patch and darn some of her own clothes then it was hardly the end of the world. She had made it through the Great Depression without a complaint. If she had to do a little bit of stitching and wash the neighbours' laundry for some extra money, then it was hardly the worst thing to happen.

Eddie didn't much care for the children. To begin with, he was awkward in their company, but as time dragged on he became actively hostile towards them. The first time that he hit one of the kids while drunk he woke up in the gutter outside with a nasty lump on the back of his head. He kept his hands to himself from that point forward, but he always felt Gert's watchful eye on him, even when he was in a stupor. He hated the way that she doted on the kids, loathed the way she would chat with them as though they were her friends rather than the nasty little leeches on her time that they really were. If he could have had Gert, and the child-support cheques, without the children then Eddie would probably have been a very content man. As it was, he spent every moment in their company sullen.

For all of his other faults, Eddie was at least good company. When he was sober and alone with Gert he was attentive and affectionate. For the first time in her adult life,

Gert came to understand that sex wasn't just a misery that women had to endure, but something that she might actually enjoy. The actual act was still something that she forced herself to play-act through, but when she did, Eddie was like putty in her hands. Men had always been dangerous to her; even when her father was still around he was as likely to shout at her as to defend her, and she had always treated the boys who she was dating like barely domesticated animals, waiting for them to turn feral at any given moment—another holdover from her mother's education on the desires of young men. It was only now that she was coming to realise that men could be tamed using exactly the same thing that her mother had always warned her they were after. She had seen a glimmer of that when she was courting attention as a teenager, but now that she was fully grown she was finally realising the potential. She managed to keep Eddie pliant and pleasant for almost three months with the cunning application of a little bit of flirtation. With a little bit more than flirtation, she managed to get him to stop drinking and get back out into the world to look for work.

Once he had an income of his own and some better prospects, he filed for divorce without even speaking to Gert about it. When they met in court his given reason for leaving her was that "the children annoyed him" and in the face of such utter lack of empathy and no counter-arguments from the stunned and furious Gert, the judge granted the divorce without any complications. The entire relationship from meeting to divorce lasted less than a year.

The child support cheques from John were still coming through intermittently, and now that they weren't being intercepted by anyone, Gert found that she could afford everything that the family needed with ease, provided that she remained thrifty. Still, there was a great deal of shame attached to being a single mother, and she found herself growing lonely in the long evenings when the children were settled in their beds. At the same time, after the humiliation of the divorce from Eddie, her confidence was too beaten to attempt another round of dating.

She bumped into John one day when he was out on patrol in the neighbourhood, entirely by accident, and the two of them immediately fell back into their old familiar rhythms of conversation. She hadn't meant to invite him over for dinner, but when there was a lull in the conversation it had felt like the appropriate thing to do. When he'd shown up on her doorstep the kids had gone into a frenzy of excitement that their father was home. Gert could remember that excitement when her own father came home. She could remember the pain of separation so acutely that it might as well have been yesterday. After dinner she plied John with a bottle of Eddie's leftover liquor until the kids were all settled and snoring in their beds, then she plied him with the new skills that she had developed in their time apart. If the kids had been delighted to see their father at dinner time, they were even happier when he was still there for breakfast. Within a few weeks, everything was settled and John had moved back in.

Their second wedding was a low-key affair, attended by only a few close family members and conducted without much ceremony. Both Gert and John seemed considerably more relaxed this time around. That sense of calm followed them back to their home, too. Finally feeling like he had the wife that he deserved, John became a better husband. Finally feeling like she had him under her thumb, Gert became a better wife.

All of that tranquillity lasted about a year before Gert became pregnant again. She had almost carried the baby to term before she miscarried. It wasn't the first time that this had happened to her, but it was the first time that it had happened so late, and she sunk into a deep depression. The house fell into disrepair, the meals became dull and tasteless, and then eventually stopped appearing on the table at all. Their love life shrivelled up and died, and every complaint that Gert ever had about her first marriage to John came back around again to haunt him. He started to hit her again, at first just to snap her out of hysterical episodes, but soon just because he felt like she deserved it. It seems that she felt the same way because she made no attempt to stop him, even needling him to the point of violence on more than a few occasions. She continued her descent into darkness until she discovered that she was pregnant once again, at which point she snapped back to her old self. John had been on the verge of leaving the house again before she got the news, and he was so pleased by the sudden change in her behaviour and demeanour that his violence immediately stopped, adding further credence in her mind to the theory that she deserved whatever punishment he had been dishing out for her being a 'bad wife.' Over the course of the next seven years, this pattern would repeat itself over and over. She would miscarry and fall into a depressive slump, then she would become pregnant again and recover. By the end of their second marriage, Gert had given birth to two healthy children. The rest had died before they could come to term. After seven years of this emotional rollercoaster, John was the one to file for their second divorce. Once again, Gert was left with full custody of all six of her children, uncontested.

Gertrude Wright

At 37 years old, Gert was an unstable single mother with six children and no income beyond what she received from her ex-husband in child support. After relying so heavily on John for financial support during their second marriage, and with the gradual degeneration of her faculties, Gert found herself unable to cover the mortgage payments on the home that she had shared with her husbands and children throughout their lives and was on the verge of eviction when she latched on to Dennis Wright as a possible saviour. Dennis was already married to someone else when she met him, and she was ten years his senior. Gert leveraged both of those power imbalances for all that they were worth, using sexual favours as a reward whenever Dennis pleased her in other ways. She moved into his home the day after his wife moved out and brought her whole brood along with her. Young Dennis was not a particularly well-adjusted individual himself, prone to self-destructive bouts of drinking that may have explained his impaired decision making when it came to his new living arrangements. Whatever power Gert had over him seemed to be effective—he shouldered the financial burdens of his suddenly expansive family without a complaint.

Gert's instability did not vanish just because she had managed to snare herself a new lover. His lovely home on East New York Street was soon caked in filth as she refused to clean up after herself or her children. She dumped food and rubbish onto the floor as she lost interest in it and on more than one occasion one of the younger children almost choked on a discarded piece of filth. Dennis was quietly horrified by the creature that he had invited into his home, but Gert's sexual domination over him wouldn't let him escape.

Dennis had spent almost a month planning his escape from Gert's clutches. He knew that if she was in the room with him—if she could lay those hands on him—then all was lost. So he planned around it; he knew that he was most pliant just after one of their 'date nights', so he waited until she had scheduled one so that his exit would be just before it. He wasn't proud of the idea of sneaking out on a household full of kids and a woman who had clearly been through too much, but this was all getting too real for him too quickly. He didn't even know if he wanted kids, let alone six of the wailing little bastards. He hadn't had any with his wife, so he certainly wasn't ready to dive into it with some woman he barely knew. He didn't have to endure for much longer, he just had to wait for Gert to start making some advances so that he knew she was in the mood, then he could pack a bag and get out of dodge. Then the rancid house, the screaming kids and she would just be a distant memory. He had family out of state, he could find a job anywhere, he didn't have to stay and suffer through a lifetime of misery with that hag just because she could lick her lips and make his knees weak.

He was ready for the usual cacophony as he walked up to the door, ready to trip over discarded soda bottles and smell the sharp tang of soaked diapers, but instead, the house was almost silent. He pushed open the door tentatively and almost gasped when he realised that he could see the carpet in the hallway again. All of the mail, newspapers and assorted crap that had formed a thick patina over the hallway had been peeled off. The base of the walls where muddy boots had splattered was now scrubbed clean and the mound of coats by the door had been squirreled away into some closet. He closed the door quietly, scared that if he made too much noise it would burst this bubble of peace that had somehow formed in his house. It actually felt like his house again—not a warren of screeching feral children or a garbage heap. He wondered for a moment if he had come in the wrong door. Then he wondered if he had gone deaf. Both worries vanished when he heard Gert in the kitchen, her voice lilting in song like something out of a Disney movie. He paced softly along the corridor, admiring the clean floors, the clean walls, the clean everything. He hadn't even realised how oppressive the filth had gotten until it was gone, and now it was like a weight had been lifted off his chest and he could breathe again. He did, drawing in lungsful of fresh, clean air and the faintest hint of bleach.

He was grinning by the time that he reached the kitchen and the warm aromas of a homecooked dinner joined the mix. Gert was by the stove, singing away to the children gathered around the table and lounging around the counters. Judging by the state of their faces they had already eaten before he arrived, which was lucky because Gert turned to him with a startlingly bright smile. She looked like a different person. The sunken eyes, the sneer, it was all gone. The woman that she pretended to be in those moments when they were tumbling in the sheets and he was losing control of his life, that was the woman who was standing in his kitchen right now, cooking him his dinner and looking like the perfect picture of a pristine housewife. He would never have known that until yesterday her clothes were filthy and crusted with sweat. He couldn't have even guessed at the horrific state of his house before today if he looked at it now. But of course, he wasn't looking at it because he only had eyes for Gert. She drifted over and planted a soft kiss on his lips and he couldn't even stop smiling long enough for that. 'Welcome home, Dennis. Dinner will be ready in just a moment. Why don't you grab a seat.'

She shooed the kids away with a wave of her hand and they all filed out, with a few of them casting resentful looks back. He was pretty sure he could smell peach cobbler in the oven, so he could understand that jealousy.

The meal was delicious, but it was nothing compared to the way that Gert was looking at him, or just the way that she looked. It was like somebody had turned the clock back on her sad life and she was back to being young and beautiful again. She smiled easily and batted her eyelids whenever he complimented her, and he found that he just couldn't stop complimenting her because everything was so sweet in that moment. She came around to sit on his lap after he was finished eating and wiped at the corner of his mouth with a napkin. 'I'm sorry I haven't been treating you right, Dennis, but I promise that all that is changing now.'

'Yeah?' He grinned.

Her hands slipped over his chest and up around the back of his neck. Her eyes filled up his vision, huge and heavy-lidded like a cow's. He wet his lips. 'Oh yeah.'

'I've been dreadful to you, and I want to start making it up to you tonight.' She shifted slightly on his lap and with a shiver, he realised just what making it up to him might look like. In the back of his mind, a little voice was screaming that he had a plan—that he was getting out—but he quashed it without a second thought. That was before she changed. Now everything was going to be all right.

Hours later he fell back onto his side of the bed, slick with sweat and aching with effort. It was a good pain, the kind of pain that leaves you well aware of just how alive you are. In the moonlight he could see Gert stretched out across the bed, her skin shimmering in the blue tint. Her laugh came out in a throaty rumble and his was so low it was almost a growl. 'You starting to forgive me yet?'

He let out a noise that could only be described as a giggle. 'I just might, at that. I just might.'

She leaned over and the little sheet that was covering her fell away. He felt a familiar stirring at the bottom of his stomach. Her eyes widened when she noticed him twitching. 'Again, already? Are you trying to wear me out?'

'Takes more than two tumbles to put you to sleep.' He smirked back.

'Not so fast now, we've got some things to discuss first.'

He rolled over and started to crawl towards her. 'Better discuss them fast, because here I come.'

'Well, there is a certain order to things. First comes love, then comes marriage...'

He stopped crawling and his good mood started to cool just as quickly as the sweat on his back. 'You know I can't up and marry you. I'd need to get my papers in to the courthouse first and that takes time and lawyer money.'

She wiggled across the bed in a very distracting fashion until they were close enough to kiss. 'I just think that we should get it settled sooner rather than later is all. Because... you never know what might happen.'

The cold had settled into Dennis' bones by now. 'What is that supposed to mean?'

'I just mean... well you do know where babies come from, right? You aren't that young.'

His stomach turned over and in an instant, all of the dull dread he had been pushing to the back of his mind came bursting back in like an unwelcome house guest. 'I don't want any babies, Gert.'

She shrugged, setting things jiggling and distracting him all over again. 'Well, life doesn't much care about what we want, Dennis. We get what the Lord gives us, and we have to make do. You know that I love every one of my babies, but I didn't want a single one of them after the first. And here I am anyway.'

He was staring at her now, trying to look past the sheen of sweat and the distracting flesh and focus on the woman behind it all. He met her eyes and tried to push all her tricks to one side. His eyes darted down to her stomach. Was it looking fuller than before? Was it just the filling meal that they had shared? Was she... His fist had clenched before he had time to think. 'Are you telling me something?'

'Well, I'd hoped that we could talk about our plans—'

'Have you got a baby in your gut?' He growled over her whispers. 'Have you?'

For a moment that calm confidence on her face wavered and he could see the sunken-eyed hag staring out at him again. The nightmare that had ruined his house, ruined his life and had plans to ruin his future too. A baby. There would be no coming back from that. She would have her hooks in him forever if she had a baby. He had seen what she had done to the cop that she had been running around with before. He would be paying out of his nose until the day he died. He would never be able to escape. A state over or the other side of the country. It wouldn't matter once his name was on that birth certificate. He reared back from Gert like she was a venomous snake. 'I don't want any babies!'

She smiled at him indulgently and rubbed a hand over her stretch-marks. 'Maybe should have thought of that before you—'

His fist caught her in the cheek, hard enough to draw blood. She didn't even cry out. She had too much experience at taking beatings for that; he had seen her scars. Instead, she just looked surprised. A little bit disappointed. He hit her again, this time in the eye, which snapped her head back with a satisfying thump.

He was not going to have a baby. She was not going to get her hooks in him. He was going to get free. He rained blows down on her and she lifted her bare arms up to fend the worst off from her face. He almost took delight in driving his fists into her chest, watching the gentle curves of her body darken and bruise under his assault.

It was only when he started to hammer his knuckles down into her stomach that anything like a rational thought even crossed his mind. He didn't have to have a baby. She couldn't do this to him. He wouldn't let her do this to him. He hit her there, again and again, at some point she had started to scream and cry. Now she was begging him. 'Not the baby. Please. Anything but the baby.'

He almost left the bed as he drew his fists up and hammered them down again. And again. There was blood on his hands and there was blood on the sheets, but it wasn't enough. He wanted the baby out of her. He wanted it broken and gone. He didn't care if it was a baby. He didn't care if it was right or wrong. He wasn't going to let her do this to him.

The blood didn't come until later, and it wasn't as much as Gert had been expecting. The pregnancy was too early for it to be much, but it was still a sure sign that Dennis had gotten his way. She lost the baby in the early hours of the next morning while Dennis lay snoring contentedly in their bed. She sat there on the toilet, hollow-eyed, and felt all of the joy and life draining out of her body.

The relationship limped on after that. Gert unwilling to give up her claim on him and Dennis too weak-willed to wrench himself free from her dubious charms. She'd kept up appearances since the pregnancy. Kept the house spotless and the children well behaved. He had a hot meal on the table every night when he got in from work and she was more than willing to leap into bed with him at a moment's notice. It should have made him suspicious, but he just wasn't that smart. She didn't let him know that she was pregnant until he managed to work it out for himself and this time he accepted it with dull complacency. Gert genuinely believed that she had won him over, body and soul.

When the baby came she named it Dennis Junior. When she returned home from the hospital the father had vanished into the night.

Of all the degradations and embarrassments that Gert had suffered in her life, this one was the most brutal. There was no trace of Dennis left behind, not even his name. She claimed to anyone who would listen that Dennis had married her before he left. That the baby wasn't a bastard. That she was a widow. She rattled through different lies so quickly that she often switched stories in the midst of a conversation with a single neighbour. Whatever had rooted Gert in reality before had now come untethered. She stopped eating and only drank when one of the older children put a bottle of soda into her hand. Doctors came by to visit her frequently, and the talk of the neighbourhood was that she was suffering from chronic illnesses. She went from looking like a relatively pretty middle-aged woman to looking skeletal within a few weeks as if Dennis Junior were sucking the very life out of her.

The rumours circulated quickly enough, and once again in her life that network of whispers among the women nearby actually served to help Gert. She was asked to babysit on many occasions and paid generously for her efforts. Women who had managed their household workloads effortlessly throughout their adult lives suddenly needed to pass some of their washing to her to clean and iron because they just couldn't manage anymore, and she was such a dear for helping them out. More cash changed hands. John's child support payments were few and far between. He had learned about Dennis, about the comfortable home that Gert was nesting in, and he had decided that she didn't need his hard-earned money anymore. There was rent to pay on the house and children to feed and clothe, so she went through the motions despite it all meaning nothing to her.

Paula Baniszewski

While Gert was going through all of her various dramas and traumas, time had not stood still for her children. Her eldest daughter Paula had been forced into the role of friend and confidant to her mother since a very young age, learning all of the gruesome details of her one constant parental figure's life second-hand, after Gert had applied her own peculiar lens to events. She grew up with a fairly warped understanding of the world, with her understanding of romantic relationships being heavily coloured by the way that her mother interacted with men, which Paula of course saw as perfectly normal. Her teenage dating life had been less successful than Gert's. In part, this was because the sexual revolution had arrived by the time she was a teen, and as such every other girl her age was considerably more willing to be wooed. She also lacked the desperation that her mother had experienced at that age. She didn't need attention and affection. She received plenty of that from her mother, even if it came in the form of a far too familiar friendship rather than a normal parental relationship.

When Gert had her breakdown following her abandonment by Dennis, that support system vanished for all of her children, and for the first time, Paula found herself looking outside of her family for love. This began with befriending all of the neighbourhood children and school mates that she could get close to. With her mother completely checked out of reality, Paula found herself the de facto head of the household, and she used the extremely limited resources that provided to her fullest advantage. The 'Wright' house became a local hotspot for the teenagers, where they were free to smoke, listen to music and lounge around without fear of parental supervision. On the few occasions that Gert resurfaced from her room, she played along with the laidback attitude that Paula had painted her with. Gert remained unable to distinguish what was appropriate for adults to say and do around teenagers, trapped in a constant state of arrested development since her own teenage years by the isolation of her abusive relationships. Still, Paula's friendships and the expansive social network that she was growing wasn't enough for her.

Paula's date was only a year younger than her, and while she normally wouldn't have bothered with a kid like that, she couldn't deny that he had a boyish charm to him. A record was still playing in the living room and the chatter of the usual crowd almost drowned it out. She wasn't worried about anyone spotting her kissing a boy. They were all too wrapped up in their own melodramas to give her a second thought, even if she was ostensibly the hostess. When his hands slipped down to squeeze her backside Paula jumped as if she had touched a hot stove, then she pressed back into it and returned his open-mouthed mauling with the same. Every time he squeezed her, she could feel her heart thumping harder. With a giggle, she broke away and with one last nervous glance towards the living room, she took him by the hand and dragged him into her bedroom. Technically she had to share it with the other girls, but they were all chattering away in the other room. No prying eyes or hoots and hollers were going to be coming their way.

They stumbled over some old worn out shoes and nearly fell into a heap of old broken toys, but they made it to Paula's bed without any further incident. She had seen her mother with men often enough to know how this was meant to go. She guided the boy's hands up to her chest and moaned as loudly as she dared, even though it mainly hurt when the boy got too excited and mashed her breasts in his blunt fingers. She struggled out of her blouse and he was fiddling with his belt, eyes wide and mouth hanging open in anticipation. She leaned in to kiss him again with half of her buttons undone and it only took him a second to remember what he was meant to be doing. Paula was starting to feel warm. The sounds from the other room were fading away until all that she could hear was the boy's panting breath and the thunder of her own heartbeat in her ears. The door creaked open, but Paula was so lost in the moment that she didn't even realise anyone else was in the room when the screech began. 'Sinners!'

Paula leapt off the boy and tried to scramble away but her mother caught her by her hair and dragged her back. 'You filthy whore. In my house. My house!'

With a jerk of her arm, she drew a strangled yelp out of Paula and drove her to her knees. 'And you! Don't ever let me see you sniffing around my girls again. You hear me, you piece of trash. Get yourself out of this house before I do something I'll regret.'

The last few weeks had not been kind to Gert. Her hair had begun to recede and the lack of nutrition had made her eyes sink even deeper into the skull-like mask of her face. She looked like a nightmare made flesh at the best of times, but here in the deep shadows with her voice shrieking, it was lucky that Paula's date didn't wet himself as he scrambled to escape without even granting her a sympathetic glance back. Gert stormed out after him, screaming at the top of her lungs, banishing the children from her house with one long tirade of vile insults and curses. Paula was left kneeling in the darkness with tears streaming down her face and any joy from her first kiss long forgotten in the tide of terror that had just swept through her life.

Any attempt by Paula to date was met with similar outbursts and disruptions to her social routine. After the first incident, Gert removed every internal door in the house and had the older boys chop them up for firewood. The next time that she saw Paula talking with a boy alone, her happy-go-lucky façade slipped once again and she dragged the girl inside for a long lecture about how she was going to ruin her life, getting knocked up outside of marriage, destroying her prospects. When that lecture didn't work, and Paula was caught coming in late with her lips pink and swollen from kissing, Gert began crafting rules for the family for the first time in her life. Every Sunday they would attend church and for the rest of the week, it infused her lectures with new hellfire and brimstone. It wasn't enough that Paula was going to ruin her life, but she was going to tarnish her immortal soul, too. The lectures became infrequent before long, then Gert slipped back into her old habits. None of the kids had dared to confront her with the truth of her own sinful behaviour. She still called herself Mrs Wright to deflect any suggestions of impropriety, but everyone in the neighbourhood knew the truth, which meant that all of their kids knew the truth, too. None of them were willing to insult Gert by talking about them, whether because of her wild temper, because they pitied her or because they appreciated the things that she did for them – but they all knew her shame and she loathed them for it.

For Paula's part, she moved her dating life out of the line of fire with as much subtlety as a teenager can manage. She knew that like her mother her only real hope for a comfortable life was to marry well, but like her mother her taste was questionable and her patience was extremely finite. Rather than waiting for a boy her own age to establish himself and ask her out, Paula started sneaking out in the evenings and frequenting the local bars, where rumours of her presence were less likely to trickle back to her mother. It didn't take her long to snare a successful local business owner, and if he were thirty years older than her that hardly mattered in the grand scheme of things. He took her to motels and they slept together regularly for about a month before she broached the subject of marriage, since he didn't seem inclined to talk about it. That was when he took his wedding ring out of his pocket and slipped it back onto his finger. Paula may not have been taught much in the way of morals from her mother, but she had some sense of personal pride. She told him what she thought of him and left him alone in that motel room without a backwards glance.

It only took a month or two for her to realise that something was wrong, and despite all of the troubles that she had gone through with her mother since she started trying to date there was never any question in her mind that Gert was the only one that could help her. They took the bus to the doctor's office while one of the neighbourhood mothers watched the young ones and the rest of the kids were off to school and a quick blood test confirmed what they already knew—Paula was pregnant.

It was the final straw for Gert. Already close to breaking point, seeing her daughter repeating exactly the same mistakes that she had made was enough to push her over the edge into full mania. With the work of all the older children the house had been kept liveable up until that point, and through a silent agreement they had forced enough food into their mother to keep her from dying, but now Gert went beyond her usual catatonic state into viciousness. If she caught the children doing housework she would chase them out. If they tried to feed her, she would scream at them until they gave up. Where before, she would put up with any amount of silliness and roughhousing in her living room, now she actively encouraged it, spreading rumours amongst the neighbourhood children with a delight and viciousness that startled even the most hardened of the usual snide commentators. Where before she had lived in squalor because she was too lost to the world to do anything about it, now she revelled in the gruesome state of her hovel and the depths of misery that she had sunk to.

The Likens Arrangement

Paula pressed on with her life as though her mother weren't in the midst of a complete nervous breakdown. Her dating life ground to a halt with the pregnancy but she had managed to keep it a secret from the neighbourhood kids and even most of her brothers and sisters, so her social life didn't suffer. Their house had become the social hub for all the teenagers in the neighbourhood long before this latest collapse in standards, but now it was the only place to be. Teenagers were not perturbed by the mess, and the fact that Gert not only let them do whatever they wanted but actively joined in with their petty squabbles was amazingly entertaining to the kids.

Still, even Paula needed a break from being in that house sometimes, and even though the majority of her friends congregated there every day after school, occasionally she managed to slip out and visit one of the ones who had decided not to. Darlene McGuire was from an Irish family who were just slightly on the wrong side of respectable and Gert had treated her to a few searing comments as a result. She would still come around the house fairly often, but it wasn't a daily occurrence for her as it was for so many of the others.

Darlene was a nice girl with a mess of curly black hair, and Paula didn't have enough nice in her life. If there was a nasty rumour going around town, you wouldn't hear it from her, and if the church was doing a charity drive Darlene would give her last penny because she wanted to help, not just because she was trying to keep up appearances like all the rest of them. Her only bad habit was taking in strays. Her mother had to forcibly evict several cats and dogs over the years, along with a handful of birds and, on one memorable occasion, a possum. The latest pair of strays that she had picked up were introduced to Paula as Sylvia and Jenny Likens. Sylvia looked to be about Paula's age, as pretty as anyone Paula had ever met, soft-spoken but friendly. Jenny was a little bit younger and lot more awkward than her sister. She had leg braces strapped on over her clothes, a reminder of a bout of childhood Polio that she had never quite recovered from. Darlene had found them wandering around town and dragged them home with her when it became clear that they had nowhere to go.

With a little bit of wheedling and cajoling, all four girls headed back to Paula's house. They settled in her room to listen to some records and drink soda while the older girls smoked and tried to pry the story out of the younger two. It all came out after an hour or so, with each of the Likens girls contributing her share reluctantly.

In the middle of the night, Betty had shaken her daughters awake. She had a bag packed for each of them. A crazed look shimmered in her eyes and there was a bruise around one of them. She spoke in hissing whispers. 'Come on girls, we're getting out of here. I'll not spend another night under the same roof as that bastard.'

They had stumbled around in the dark getting into their clothes, and after a couple of attempts, Betty managed to get Jenny's braces snapped into place without nipping her. Together they all snuck out into the dimly lit street, and for a brief moment when the cold night air hit her face, Sylvia wondered when this strange dream was going to end. They made it to the bus station before the reality of it had started to sink in, and Sylvia was wondering if she could make a break for it back to her father. Lester wasn't a particularly terrible father any more than Betty was a terrible mother—they were just intensely and deeply self-involved. Their relationship had taken centre stage throughout their entire lives. Their daughters were just set dressing.

If Sylvia had run back to him he would have continued to be a thoroughly average father and Betty would vanish into the night just like she had planned. Life could stay the same, more or less, if she just found the courage to stand up and run home. Jenny met her eyes. She was perched on the edge of the row of plastic bucket seats opposite Sylvia and she looked like she was ready to cry. Sylvia could have abandoned her mother to whatever bizarre adventure she had planned, but she couldn't leave Jenny to suffer through it alone. She just couldn't. Together, grasping tightly to their sparse luggage and each other's hands, the girls boarded a bus to Indianapolis and hoped for the best.

The bus smelled faintly of urine, and the only other people on it were frankly terrifying to Sylvia. A wild-eyed man with a bushy beard occupied the back seat, surrounded by empty beer cans. An old lady who didn't seem to be breathing had her head resting against the window near to the front. The sisters slipped into a seat together behind their mother, and Sylvia didn't complain once even though Jenny seemed to be doing her level best to crush every bone in her hand. As the bus rumbled along, the sharp pangs of terror started to dull and the realisation that it was still the middle of the night settled on them heavily. Jenny was the first to drift off, her snores a gentle whisper in Sylvia's hair. Next, her mother slumped forward over her overstuffed purse and started to drool. Sylvia was the last to fall asleep, nervousness jerking her back to attention every time that the bus rattled but exhaustion dragging her back down again just as quickly.

They arrived in Indianapolis before the sun came up, gathered their cases from beneath the bus and headed out into the town with 'fresh hope in their hearts'—according to Betty. Unfortunately, the fresh hope in their hearts was not matched by cash in their purses. Betty had spent everything that she had with her on the bus tickets and now their grand adventure was coming to an abrupt end before it had even begun. Sylvia was stoic, but it didn't take Jenny long to complain about missing breakfast. Betty's eyes had lighted up with misguided romantic notions about caring for her babies now that they were all alone in the world, and a few minutes later the girls were waiting outside of a minimarket while their mother went in to steal them something to eat. Sylvia was practically vibrating with tension, even before the police car pulled up in front of the building. When Betty was led out in cuffs, Sylvia had to drag Jenny away so that she didn't give them away and have them all dragged off to jail. The girls had spent the rest of the day rambling around the city aimlessly until Darlene had found them and taken them home.

Paula was rather taken with all of the drama in the story, and while she had now come to find Jenny to be dull as dishwater, Sylvia seemed like she could be a friend. It was with that friendship in mind that she walked down the hallway to her mother's room where she lay like a corpse, unmoving in her bed, and asked if the two girls could stay the night, paraphrasing the story of their escape from an abusive husband in the hopes of stirring some empathy in the dead-eyed woman. Gert crept through to meet the girls with a grin plastered over her face that made Jenny shiver. 'You lovely girls are welcome to stay the night. Of course you are. Don't you worry, we will take good care of you and in the morning we will find out where your mother has gotten to. Don't you worry about a thing."

There was so much warmth forced into those words that even the ever-sceptical Sylvia didn't doubt them. She thanked "Mrs Wright" profusely until the woman stopped her with a giggle. 'Just call me Mom dear, everybody does. All the little boys and girls who come through that door.'

The Likens girls slept in Paula's bed that night after Darlene had gone home, and after the exhausting ordeal of the previous day, they slept through until almost lunchtime when a hammering on the door woke everyone in the house. Gert slunk through in her nightgown and jerked the door open, expecting some fool of a door-to-door salesman. Instead, she came face to face with Lester Likens, and just behind him Darlene McGuire.

Darlene had met Lester roaming the streets searching for his daughters. He had been called when his wife was put into the county jail and the subject of bail came up. All of the paperwork was already being processed and Betty would be released before the end of the day. Their brief separation and the anguish that they had both felt was enough to drive them to reconcile, and through the plate glass of the visiting room at the jail the two had renewed their pledges of love and loyalty to one another and started to make plans for the future. Plans that once again centred their romantic notions and left their daughters on the periphery.

Lester gave Gert a gap-toothed grin and started to explain. He had friends who were working the touring carnival circuit and making really good money, and both Betty and Lester had been offered a place with one that was just about to head south. Unfortunately, there was no room for kids in the carnival. The girls had rushed out to greet their father once they knew that he had arrived, and they were relieved to hear that his problems with Betty were, at least temporarily, at an end. They were a little taken aback at his plan to abandon them, however. He switched immediately to the wheedling voice that he usually used when he had angered their mother. Talking about what a great opportunity it was for them. About how it would let them save up for a better future for the girls. They were unconvinced, but they weren't the one that Lester's pleading was meant to convince. In the end, he turned to Gert and outright asked her if she would keep the girls for him. Giving them room and board in exchange for twenty dollars a week. Twenty dollars a week would keep Gert in cigarettes for the rest of her life, and regular, guaranteed money was a rarity in her house. She took very little convincing before she agreed to take the girls on. With the number of children already in her house, she joked that she probably wouldn't even notice a couple more.

With everything agreed on her doorstep, Lester shook hands with Gert and went off to make arrangements for the rest of the girls' belongings to be passed along. Not once did he step inside and see the horrific state of disrepair in the house. Nor did he cast a glance around for long enough to realise that there were half as many beds as there were people living there. He was just delighted that he was going to be able to rush off into the sunset with his darling wife once more. Inside the house, Paula made a show of being happy that the new girls were moving in, telling Sylvia that now they were going to be like sisters, but already she was uncomfortable having these strangers living with her. In normal circumstances, she probably would have genuinely embraced these two lost souls, but circumstances were anything but normal, and she had a massive secret that she was trying to keep under wraps. One that would be almost impossible to conceal from a pair of girls her own age who were going to be sharing her living space.

The Missed Payment

For the first week of their strange new tenancy, the Likens girls were bemused by the strangeness of 'Mom' and the packed household of neighbourhood children. In a way, it seemed almost like a teenage utopia with no rules except the ones that they chose to abide by themselves. Sadly, like so many periods of anarchy throughout history, this resulted in a horrible hierarchy of social Darwinism where the strong preyed on the weak. The Baniszewski kids all held some measure of power in the circle by virtue of it being their home, with the older girls Paula and Stephanie holding the lion's share. Whichever boy seemed to have their preference at any given moment also gained a measure of respect and power, with Stephanie's sporadic boyfriends leaping to the head of the pack. Gert oversaw all the infighting with an impartial eye, only intervening if it looked like the situation might turn against her children, and even then, only when she felt like things were getting out of control. Even in this chaos, there were certain rituals that she still forced the family to observe. They attended the church every Sunday, and if there were other events being held there through the week she scrubbed every child down and sent them along. She was aware of how tentative her grasp on respectability was and had long ago discovered that having the church vouch for her was a good way to avoid having to actually make any personal improvements.

The Likens girls had perfect attendance at the local school, once again enforced by Gert with the same quiet fury that she used to keep everyone attending church. Even when Jenny was in pain because of her legs, she still attended without fail. Truancy was another sign of impropriety which Gert would not tolerate. She was desperate to keep her personal situation hidden, even though so many people had already learned about it through the whisper mill of neighbourhood gossip. The Likens girls seemed to get on well in school, achieving academically and making friends easily. The Baniszewski clan had considerable sway within the school, and the fact that Paula was willing to vouch for the new girls went a long way towards establishing their social credibility.

It was after a pleasant day of school that the Likens girls returned home to find the place bizarrely quiet. All of the usual after school crowd were absent, with only the Baniszewski kids themselves still lingering around. Thinking that they had stumbled onto some new family ritual that they knew nothing about, they tried to make themselves scarce until they could ask Paula what was going on. In the room that the four girls shared, Paula was waiting, but so was Gert. Without a word, the two women seized a hold of Sylvia and forced her face-down onto the pallet of dirty clothes that she had been forced to use as a bed. Gert was roaring and screaming. 'I took care of you two little bitches for nothing! Lie down there! Lie down.'

She scrambled on top of Sylvia and hauled down her skirt and her underwear while Paula giggled, then she hefted a stirring stick from the kitchen and began to beat Sylvia's bare backside, the girl screaming the whole time. Jenny was frozen with terror, trapped in a moment of indecision between running for her life and trying to help her sister. She didn't get a chance to make the choice. Paula grabbed her and threw her down on the makeshift bed beside Sylvia, wrestling to get her underwear and her skirts down and getting them hopelessly tangled in Jenny's leg braces. Gert rained blows down on Jenny's backside too, then started beating her way down the girl's already aching thighs, drawing wails of anguish out of the girl.

'Your no-good lying rat of a father promised me that he would pay his way. It's been a week and I ain't seen a God damned penny from him. I've been feeding you and washing you and putting a roof over your head and raising you right and that bastard hasn't even sent me a measly dollar. Twenty dollars a week. That is what we agreed. Twenty dollars. A pittance. To keep his darling daughters safe and well. Well, you ain't going to be safe and well. Not if I ain't going to get my twenty dollars! Do you bitches hear me? If he don't pay, you get beat!'

The blows continued to rain down on the girls and it seemed like the more that they cried out, the more excitable Gert became. On a backswing, she smashed a mirror, and when Paula stepped forward with a cry of dismay she caught the stick across her knuckles, too. 'Mom!'

Gert slowed and stopped, trailing the tip of the stick over the curve of Sylvia's red raw backside with visible delight. Gert's breathing was as ragged as the sobs that were still slipping out of Sylvia. She leaned down close and hissed into the teenager's ear. 'If your daddy hasn't paid what he is meant to by tomorrow you're going to get it again. If he hasn't paid by the end of the week then I am renting you girls out at a dollar a ride until I make my money. You hear me, whores?'

Sylvia moaned out, 'Yes!' and that seemed to be enough to satisfy Gert. She stalked out of the room with a sneer still on her face. Paula left a moment later, pushing through the crowd of her younger brothers who had gathered in the doorway to get their first good look at what a girl looked like with no clothes on.

The humiliation stung the girls almost as badly as the beating that they had just taken. The next day, Sylvia had to help Jenny limp into school with every step drawing a tear to their eyes. Paula strolled on ahead of them with a superior smirk still on her face. Lester's cheque arrived that same morning, accidentally delayed by the postal service as it crossed state lines.

There was never much to eat in the house. Gert kept the cupboards bare, sending one of the older kids out to fetch in something simple when she herself got hungry enough, which was rarely. It didn't take long before the Likens girls went foraging to help supplement the occasional meals that they were receiving. They had discovered that they could trade discarded Cola bottles in at the local store for credit, so one day after school they went out foraging and after scouring the nearby streets, they had gathered enough to buy themselves some candy. They ate a fair portion of it on their walk back to the house, but Sylvia insisted that they save some for the Baniszewski children, whom she still felt a great deal of sympathy for, despite the way that they had revelled in her humiliation.

Gert caught them handing the sweets out and immediately another fury overtook her. She accused the girls of stealing the candy, and when Sylvia tried to explain how they had earned the money to buy it, she was dragged back through to her bedroom and thrown down for another beating. This time Jenny had the good sense to stay silent and out of the way, but Paula and Stephanie both came in to watch the show as Sylvia's underwear was hauled off again and she was paddled with a wooden spoon while Gert chanted, 'Thief! Liar! Thief! Liar!' over and over. She pinned Jenny in place with a stare. 'Are you going to lie to me too, little thief? Here I am, doing everything for you and this is how you repay me? Well, little liar? Where are your lies? What's your story? Come on, little thief, tell us your story!'

With every outburst, she unleashed another searing strike across the back of Sylvia's thighs. Each sneering demand was punctuated by another scream. 'Answer me, you lying little bitch! Tell me the truth!'

Jenny could hardly speak through her sobbing, at least until Paula grabbed her ponytail and jerked her head back. 'It's... it's like you said. We stole the candy. We stole it. Please... please stop.'

Gert hammered the spoon into Sylvia's back with a squeal of victory. 'I knew it! I knew you were a nasty little liar.'

She grabbed the back of Sylvia's hair and dragged her face up so that she could see the tears streaming down the girl's face and the terror in her eyes. 'If you ever lie to me again it will be the last time. Do you hear me, you filthy little bitch? Do you hear me?!'

Sylvia hissed out between her gritted teeth, 'Yes.'

Just as suddenly as all the madness had begun, it was over. Gert stormed back out of the room with Paula trailing out behind her, shaking her head in mock shame as she left. Jenny rushed to her sister's side and cradled her as Sylvia sobbed pitifully. Only her sister heard her whispering. 'I just wanted to do something nice.'

The Hotdog

Sylvia and Jenny were on their best behaviour from that moment forward. Which meant that they tried to fade into the background and go completely unnoticed. All of Sylvia's friends at school watched as she drew away from them and became quiet. The neighbourhood kids who had initially taken such an interest in her now judged her to be just as dull as her sister, and they were side-lined. The girls avoided Gert as completely as possible, realising that the only way to be safe from her bizarre accusations was to stay out of sight. But even that proved insufficient to protect them from Gert's ever-deepening madness.

One night after school the church had a raffle that the Baniszewski children were all sent to attend while their mother lay in bed—to maintain her presence in the community without her having to move. It was a dull affair as usual, but the Likens sisters were secretly delighted. Reverend Julian was a simpering man, quite unlike the fire and brimstone preachers that they had encountered on the road with their parents, but he seemed to genuinely care for the wellbeing of all of his parishioners, which meant that he could be relied on to sneak them a little bit of food as charity every time he saw them. He had watched their weight loss over the course of the last few months, and he had been informed through the grapevine that even though money was tight in the Baniszewski household, kindly Gertrude had invited these orphans to live with them. It was the least that he could do to provide them with a small share of the buffet meal that he had laid on from the edible donations.

It had been three days since the Likens girls had eaten, and they were shaky and weak. Sylvia had to stop her sister from stuffing her face on several occasions. Painfully aware of the pitying looks that the other attendees were giving them and determined not to draw any attention to them, she limited herself to sandwiches spaced out over the course of the low-key event. That and one little chocolate cake slice that Reverend Julian slipped into her hand when he was saying goodbye. She held onto her sister's arm on the way home, helping to support her when the usual weakness in her legs combined with the malnutrition to drag her to a halt.

Once they were back to the house, Sylvia tucked Jenny into bed and tried to settle her before the usual ruckus from the living room got so loud that it woke her up. Gert didn't seem to object to the girls sleeping. Anything that kept them out of sight seemed to please the old woman. Sylvia took a long hard look at her own "bed." If she stayed here then there would be no barbed comments, and no chance for 'Mom' to punish her from some new imagined slight. But the music and laughter in the living room sounded just a little too tempting. Sylvia decided that she deserved some good things in her life, even if she could only have them from the periphery.

When she came out into the hall, the living room fell silent. With dull dread she plodded through to see Gert sitting in the midst of the children, holding court. 'And here comes the little piggy now.'

There weren't many of the neighbourhood kids lounging around tonight. The church social hadn't been quite cool enough for most of them, and with the Baniszewski house empty except for Gert they felt a little awkward. Gert's kids were enough to fill the small room to bursting all on their own, of course. The little ones started making little oinking noises until Gert silenced them with a glare. "I hear that you're out bringing shame on me again."

Sylvia wondered if she could run back to her room, but it wouldn't help—there were no doors. The crowd could just come pouring in and drag her back out to stand trial. 'I don't know what you mean... Mom.'

She couldn't often bring herself to use the title that Gert had chosen for herself, but it always seemed to make the matriarch of this wretched clan happy when she did.

Sylvia could tell from the predatory stares that she was getting from Paula and Stephanie that she needed all the help she could get right now. Gert's face was still and hard as stone. 'Why are you so disgusting?'

The little ones started to giggle at that. Sylvia had no idea what to say to that, so she stared down at the scuffed tops of her shoes.

'Did you think that nobody was going to notice you stuffing your face, pig? Did you think that my beautiful children had no eyes in their heads? Did you think that the whole neighbourhood wasn't talking about how you took all of the food that was meant for everyone and stuffed it down your filthy throat? Do you know what they're whispering now? They're whispering that old Gert doesn't take care of those children. That I starve you. Why do you want to shame me so badly? Why would you do that? Were you raised by animals? Did you grow up in a pigsty, nursing from a sow?'

Sylvia could already feel tears pricking at her eyes. Her stomach ached with hunger, even after the extra treat that the reverend had slipped her. She was always hungry now. Hunger and fear took turns to make her stomach ache, but the pain was constant. It made her do stupid things, such as answering back. 'I didn't... I wouldn't.'

Gert jerked upright in the chair. 'So my babies are all liars now are they? And all the good people at the church too, you're calling them all liars? When I have the Reverend come around my door banging and wailing about the sin of gluttony and how vile and debased you were, shovelling the scraps that the church provides him to eat down your maw, I am meant to believe you? I am meant to believe a filthy liar like you over a priest? Over the word of God himself, we are meant to listen to the gospel of Sylvia Likens the filthy little liar?'

'I didn't say—'

'You didn't have time to say a damned thing when you were stuffing your face with everything. You disgust me. Are you hungry Sylvie? Are you so hungry you need to shame yourself? Shame us all?'

The tears that she had been holding back began to flood down Sylvia's cheeks, but that just seemed to excite 'Mom' even more. She was straining forward in her seat and making a dreadful croaking sound, somewhere between a gasp and a laugh. Sylvia's treacherous stomach chose that moment to let out a dreadful grumble and Gert rocked back in her chair. 'Well it might not be fine dining like you are used to, but I was going to cook you something tonight. Have you still got room or have you stuffed yourself too full?!'

Sylvia shook her head again. Not ever sure what she was answering to anymore, just wanting to deny the whole situation was happening.

When she looked up Gert was out of her chair and moving. She caught Sylvia by her hair and dragged her wailing along the corridor to the filthy kitchen. She tossed her into the one chair that still had all of its legs and went to the cupboards. Gert plucked a stale bun out of one cupboard, a jar of hotdogs from another and a ragged-edged knife from a drawer. She didn't take her eyes off of Sylvia for a single moment as she sawed into the bun, shoved the cold, dripping sausage into it and marched over. 'Can't have you going hungry now, can we? Wouldn't want the whole neighbourhood to hear about how hungry poor, put-upon Sylvie is. Never working a day in her life. Wasting the best years of her life hanging around in some poor old woman's house and taking advantage of her kindness in every single way.'

'I'm sorry.'

'You're what? You're hungry? Well don't worry, dear, I've got something for you right here. Oh, wait. Wait. I can't just give you something as plain as this. That isn't good enough for little miss Sylvie. It needs to be fancy! Let's make it fancy!'

Gert pulled open the bare cupboards and dug around until she found mustard and ketchup, then she emptied almost the whole bottle of each onto the bun in her hand until it was pouring over the top and running off onto the floor. 'That is more like it. A meal fit for the fancy little princess. The poor starving Sylvia. Go on. Eat up.'

'I don't want... I can't...'

Gert rammed it into her half-closed lips and screeched. 'Eat it, you little bitch! I made it for you. You are so hungry you have to shame us all. Now eat it.'

Sylvia choked on the squirt of mustard that had made it past her closing lips and started coughing. Gert took her opportunity. She rammed the whole hotdog and bun into the girl's mouth, screaming, 'Eat it, you bitch. Eat every last bite!'

Sylvia was scrambling to get away, but Gert pushed forward until the chair hit the wall and kept ramming the hotdog in and out of the teenager's mouth, her eyes alight with some dark passion that Sylvia couldn't even begin to understand. The hotdog hit the back of her throat and she gagged, giving Gert another chance to ram it in. All the while, the woman was ranting and raving. 'Why did you do it, Sylvie? Why are you ruining that tight little body? No man is going to want you if you're fat. Nobody will ever want you if you're fat. You'll end up all alone. You are going to end up all alone in a house full of ungrateful little bastards that shame you every chance that they get. You are going to be hideous and bloated. You are going to be so fat that people laugh at you when they see you waddling down the street. Is that what you want, you rancid little bitch? You want to ruin your perfect little body by stuffing your face?"

Sylvia had no opportunity to answer. All that she could do was try to chew the mush of bread and condiments in her mouth and try not to choke on the rubbery lumps of cold hotdog before Gert pried her jaws open again to ram in some more. She had made it through half of the hotdog before nausea overtook her. The slimy ketchup was running down her face, the bright stinging taste of the mustard was burning down her throat. Her eyes were streaming with tears. What had started as an emotional breakdown had been carried on by the sharp vinegary stench of the mustard and the constant gagging. When Gert's filthy fingers went into her mouth to try to force down the latest mouthful it was too much. Sylvia choked and then retched up the noxious concoction that had just been forced into her. Gert leapt back out of the way and stared on in obvious disgust as both the hotdog and everything else that Sylvia had managed to eat that night was sprayed across the kitchen floor.

When the girl finally stopped throwing up, Gert patted her gently on the back and placed the surviving half of the hotdog in her hand. 'Just eat the rest, then you're done.'

Sylvia looked up at her with tears still streaming down her face, but whatever glimmer of empathy she hoped to find in Gert's sunken eyes just wasn't there. With shaking hands, she lifted the hotdog to her mouth and took a tentative bite. Almost immediately the foul mix of flavours—bile and mustard and sickly-sweet ketchup—had her retching again. She forced the first morsel down her throat, breathing heavily through her nose and trying to keep calm. Then she leaned forward and took another bite of the squelching mess, gulping it down despite her whole body trying to force it back out. She could do it. She could finish it. She was strong. That was what she kept on whispering to herself, in her mind. Gert looked on with barely disguised lust on her face, watching every lump sliding down Sylvia's slender neck with fearsome attention. Her fascination turned to frustration as Sylvia chewed her way through the whole gruesome meal. The girl stared up at her as she swallowed the last bite, beaming and victorious. 'I finished it!'

Gert's mouth was twisted into a comforting smile, but she shook her head. 'You did great, sweetheart, but you haven't finished yet. I told you to eat the rest.'

She gestured expansively to the spattering of vomit across the floor. Amidst the sour-smelling partially digested food it was almost too easy to pick out the pink lumps of hot dog scattered across the floor. Even without the vomit, the floor was so filthy that just the thought of eating off it was vile. Sylvia's mind just rebelled at the idea of what Gert was asking her to do. She sat in the chair, staring at the vomit and trying her hardest not to start laughing hysterically. It had to be a joke. Nobody could actually expect her to eat that. Gert tipped her out of the chair onto her hands and knees. 'Eat it, you little bitch. Eat it.'

She put her foot on Sylvia's back, between her shoulder blades, and forced her face down into the yellow tainted slime. 'Eat it!'

Sylvia closed her eyes and opened her mouth. This wasn't happening. This could not be happening. She felt something brush against her lips and it took all her strength not to retch all over again. If she was sick again then she would just have more to eat. She would have to do this all over again every time she was sick. She couldn't do it again. She kept her eyes shut and lapped at the foul-tasting fluids like she was a dog. There was so much mustard that she could hardly taste anything else. All that she had to endure was the texture and the sliminess. There was a bark of wild laughter from the doorway but Sylvia kept her eyes shut. Of course, the Baniszewski kids were watching her suffer. Of course, they were laughing. She wouldn't have expected anything less from this living nightmare. Gert had her fingers tangled in Sylvia's hair and she was leading her along the floor like a pet. Guiding her mouth to each patch of vomit. A constant litany was hissing in her ear. Gert was hunched over so close that Sylvia could feel her dry lips on the back of her neck. 'Eat every last bite. Get fat. Get so fat that nobody will ever want you. Go on, piggy. Gobble it all up. You were so pretty. You were such a pretty girl but you had to go and ruin it all. You ruined it all and now nobody wants you. You are going to be alone forever.'

Sylvia kept her eyes screwed shut tightly and tried to imagine that she was anywhere else. Doing anything else. Tasting anything else in the world. Anything except for the bitterness of bile and mustard. Even that wasn't the worst of it. The worst were the strange crunchy morsels that scratched over the roof of her mouth. The things that couldn't have been food. The things that were clearly splinters or filth that had been crusted onto the floor for months or years. Each one of those made her shudder and struggle to keep the contents of her churning stomach down, but she couldn't do this again, so she kept it all inside. Without warning it was over. Gert hauled her to her feet and stroked her hair. She smeared the mustard and ketchup off the girl's cheek with her sleeve and let out a mournful sigh. 'I only punish you because I care. You know that. If you would just be good, we could avoid all this nastiness. You've learned your lesson now, haven't you? You're never going to shame me like that again, are you? You're going to be a good girl from now on, and I'm never going to have to punish you. Wouldn't your parents be so ashamed of you if they knew what you just did? If they knew why you had to do it? They would hate you for it, wouldn't they? They wouldn't be kind to you like I am, trying to teach you a lesson so that you don't ruin your whole life.'

Paralysed with fear at what new hell Gert might inflict on her next, Sylvia nodded along with the cascade of lies as it went on and on. Like a timid lamb, she let Gert lead her to the kitchen sink and wash the filth from her face. Like someone who had been stripped of all dignity, she let Gert guide her through to the heap of dirty clothes that was now her bed and stroke her hair gently until she fell asleep, with tears running down her cheeks because it was the only thing resembling kindness she had experienced in her whole time in the Baniszewski house.

A week later—once the weight of shame and self-loathing had settled in properly—Sylvia met with her parents. Gert arranged things so that when Lester and Betty came to visit they didn't see the inside of her house. She couldn't tolerate any adult visitors, particularly when those visitors might go spreading nasty rumours around. The teenagers and the children were manageable, she had leverage over them. If they wanted to use her home as their little clubhouse then they needed to keep their nasty little mouths shut about the state of it. Since Dennis Wright abandoned her, Gert had lost any interest in men, so there was no risk of one of her dates letting her secret slip. The few neighbourhood women who used to come around to drop off their laundry or a child to be babysat now had their teenage neighbours carry it along when they were heading to visit anyway. There were no unpleasant rumours about Gert in the neighbourhood. The same pity that had always hung over her was still present, but her strange relationships with the teenagers wasn't ever subjected to scrutiny. After all, most of the parents were just relieved that they didn't have a horde of stinking teens occupying their homes.

Instead of a home visit, the Baniszewski family filled up one side of a public bus and rode to meet the Likens at Garfield Park. The meeting started off poorly. Betty was shocked at how skinny her daughters had gotten, but Gert had anticipated this line of questioning and launched into a ready-made story—explaining that the girls had both decided to go onto a diet in solidarity with her oldest daughter Paula, who had been putting on too much weight recently. As Gert lied to the Likens, one petty deception after another—painting herself as a saint—she made direct eye contact with Sylvia. She was daring the girl to challenge her. After the humiliation of the hotdog incident, the week of constant mockery at the hands of the Baniszewski children, and seeing how readily her parents were lapping up Gert's lies, Sylvia found that she couldn't. She couldn't find it in herself to fight each of these petty battles. She couldn't bear for her parents to find out what she had done, crawling around on all-fours.

Lester and Betty were delighted by the stories that Gert was telling them about their daughters, in particular about the good work that they were doing with the local church charities and the way that they were collecting cola bottles from the neighbourhood trash to make donations. Once again Sylvia received a pointed stare and nodded along glumly, flashing her mother a nervous smile when eyes turned her way. When the conversation turned to the special diet that Sylvia had been on, straying dangerously close to the awful truth of the last week, tears started to prick at her eyes and her face flushed dangerously red. Lester was mostly oblivious to the emotional lives of their daughters, but Betty saw and grabbed onto her daughter's hand. 'What is wrong, honey?'

Sylvia's tears threatened to escape. She had been doing so well. She had been keeping up appearances just like 'Mom' wanted her to and now her stupid face was going to give it all away. Luckily Gert wasn't so easily shaken. She leaned over to whisper to Betty.

'Our Sylvia is just feeling bashful because her new trim figure has been getting her a lot of attention from the gentlemen.'

Sylvia was absolutely scandalised, and the ensuing blush was intense enough to wipe any concern from her mother's mind. She fell completely silent for the rest of her parent's visit, dreading the tales that would be spun to cover up any other mistakes that she made. Jenny had missed out on the worst abuses and had been so mortified at the spanking she had received that she didn't dare to speak of it.

At the end of the visit, Betty embraced her daughters while Lester handed over an envelope of cash as an advance for the rest of the month. The carnival circuit was apparently paying well and keeping the two of them stimulated enough that they were happy together once again. Sylvia had tears in her eyes when her mother left, but even then Gert swept in to wrap an arm around her shoulders and spin a story about what a good daughter they had to miss them so much, and about how happy Sylvia was when their letters came. Neither girl had ever seen these letters but neither of them had the courage to ask.

On the bus ride home, Sylvia was seated next to 'Mom.' Gert pulled her in close and stroked her hair. Whispering softly into her ear that she had been a good girl. Petting her like she was a dog that had behaved itself well in company. 'I knew that you could be a good girl with the right discipline. I was so proud of you today. You did such a good job. You and me are going to be the best of friends now, you will see. A pretty little thing like you, why you remind me of me at that age. I had all the boys chasing after my tail too. Don't you worry though. I won't let them get you. I won't let them ruin you. Not a good girl like you.'

Being made into Gert's accomplice should have been enough to turn Sylvia's stomach, but it wasn't the most upsetting part of the day by far. The worst part was that she leaned into that touch and forced herself to believe the lies she was being told because the alternative was too horrible to contemplate.

Unfit for Chairs

The next few weeks lulled the Likens girls into a false sense of security. Gert didn't suddenly become their best friend overnight—not by any stretch of the imagination—but her outright hostility to them seemed to have ceased after they had shown that they could be trusted to uphold the lies that were the foundations of her life. With that new acceptance came a better relationship with the eldest Baniszewski girls, Paula and Stephanie. They were adept at reading their mother's moods and, for that reason, began to cosy up to the Likens girls again, starting to refer to them in casual conversations as being their adoptive sisters rather than homeless orphans. Jenny was taken in by the new overtures of friendship and became a part of their social group, on the fringes but still included in the daily activities of the hive of teens that centred around the house. Sylvia wasn't so quick to accept the girls' behaviour at face value. The abuse that she had suffered made her reluctant to join in with their casual chatter, scared of the way that her words might be twisted against her at a moment's notice, but eventually, even she succumbed to the draw of a social life and became a sitting member of the living room crowd.

Increasingly, the older girls were talking about their love lives, with Stephanie practically salivating over the thought of her new boyfriend Coy Hubbard, a fifteen-year-old regular of the Baniszewski house whom she thought was dreamy. Paula was a little more careful, talking only in the past tense about her affairs, and carefully avoiding any mention of the sexual escapades that had driven her mother over the brink into outright madness. Her pregnancy remained a secret from the Likens girls and the neighbourhood at large, but the Baniszewski kids were well aware of her delicate condition and ran interference for her, both with the boys that were interested in her and with their mother, who was particularly sensitive to the subject, preferring absolute denial to dealing with the realities of having a pregnant teenager around the house.

Jenny had admitted early on to having almost no experience with boys due to the problems that she had with her legs, leading to many of the boys in attendance offering up their services before a growl from the dozing Gert warded them off. When pressed, she mentioned that she had kissed a boy once before they moved to Indianapolis, but she couldn't even remember his name anymore. There was hooting and cheering from around the room and Sylvia found herself joining in despite herself. It was nice to have this little bit of normalcy after the craziness of the last month. Just having people she could call friends and a place where she could talk again felt like freedom. It felt like being a teenager again. She found herself appreciating Gert for giving her that back, for giving it to all of these kids—as if the bitter and twisted woman weren't the reason it had been taken from Sylvia to begin with.

Sylvia joined in with the conversation shyly at first but with a great deal of appreciation from the boys in the audience. Many of them had been extremely interested when Sylvia first came into their social circle, as she put the plain-faced Baniszewskis to shame and lacked the sharp tongue and potential ostracization that was a known danger of dating them. With more than a small amount of giggling on all sides, Sylvia talked about going steady with a boy before they had moved to Indianapolis. When pressed she admitted that they had kissed pretty often, leading to another round of whooping and cheering. With a bright smile on her lips and a flush on her cheeks, she leaned forward and stage-whispered, 'I even let him feel me up over my sweater once.'

There was rapturous applause from the boys in the audience and Paula nodded approvingly, trying to keep the smile on her face from being too obvious. Sylvia had never felt so accepted since the moment that she set foot in the "Wright" house. She turned her shy smile towards Gert, expecting the old woman to be grinning along with the rest of them, but the old woman's face was contorted into a rictus of fury and her eyes were glazed.

Gert rose up from her seat and thrust an accusatory finger at Sylvia's face. As she rose she let out a blood-curdling wail. 'Whore!'

She slapped Sylvia around the face and launched into one of her rants, eyes unseeing, spittle bubbling from her lips. 'To think that I let filth like you into my home. There is nothing in this world more detestable than a whore. That's what the Bible says. You're lower than the lowest worm. Fornicating and spreading your slime all over. All over my beautiful house. You've spoiled everything. Your life is ruined. Everyone knows you're a whore now. A filthy, filthy prostitute. How many men have you laid down with, whore? How many?'

In her panic, Sylvia forgot the lessons that her time in the Baniszewski house had taught her. She forgot to stay silent and take the abuse. She'd forgotten to let it wash over her. 'What? I've never even—'

Gert pushed her so suddenly she didn't have a chance to save herself. Her chair toppled over backwards. Before she hit the floor, her head smacked against the plaster of the wall, showering her in white dust. Gert ripped the chair out from under her and loomed, still screaming at the top of her lungs.

'Everybody knows now! You're a prostitute! A filthy whore. Everybody knows that you let a boy touch you. Why didn't you listen? I was trying to save you. Now you're never going to be anything more than a whore for all the rest of your days. You've sullied yourself. You're unclean. There's none so base as a filthy whore. Gather round children. Look at her. Look at the whore in your midst.'

The neighbourhood kids had frozen when Gert first started up, but now they cast nervous glances at each other and started to giggle. There was something a little nerve-wracking about audience participation, but at the end of the day, they knew that this was all just like a rollercoaster ride— they would get all the thrills of real danger without anyone really getting hurt.

Gert seemed to be just warming up. As the dazed Sylvia pulled herself up onto her elbow, the old woman stomped on her crotch. 'Filthy whore. We all heard what you said. It won't be long before the whole world knows it too. Any day now they're all going to see the signs. They're all going to know!'

Sylvia yelped in pain. 'What?!'

'Everyone is going to know you're a prostitute when your belly starts to swell up. When your gut grows and your skin stretches. When that poison he squirted inside you makes you sick every morning. Everyone is going to know you're a whore just by looking at you, you filthy, filthy thing. Didn't you even know? Are you stupid as well as a whore?'

'I've never. I'd never…' Sylvia squealed as Gert ground her heel down.

'Everybody knows. There's no point lying about it anymore. You let a boy touch you down there. Let him put his dirty parts inside you and now you're spoiled. You're ruined. Won't be long now until everyone can see that you're pregnant, then your misery will really start. That will be your life over and done. The minute you squirt your filthy little bastard out onto my floor it'll latch onto you and never let go.' Gert's eyes were bulging out of her head. Her teeth were gnashing between each word. She'd never looked less human. 'Whoever you were going to be—whatever your dreams were —you've ruined them all just for some boy. Some man you can't even remember the name of. You've ruined everything for some man who paid you to lie down with him.'

The old woman's eyes flicked from side to side as she concocted the new reality, then she stamped her foot down again, setting Sylvia screaming. "You're nothing but a prostitute and you'll never be anything more. You took money from a man so you could buy more sweets to stuff your face. Then he stuffed you. Oh, you wanted to fatten up. Eat me out of house and home. Ruin your figure by gobbling up all the treats your whoring money could buy. Well, you've not even started yet. You've not even begun to see how vile and bloated that putrid little pink worm in your guts is going to grow. They'll see you coming from the other end of town.'

The neighbourhood kids were cracking up. Gert's own children looked a little put out by the ranting about how having children ruined your life, but it didn't take long for them to get back on board when Gert stopped talking and started kicking. She hammered her heel into Sylvia's crotch and when the girl tried to pull her knees together the old hag hissed. 'Too late for that now. Should have kept your legs together before it was too late. You filthy whore.' She growled at the nearest boys. 'Spread her legs for her. Don't worry about hurting her. You know she likes it like that. You know she likes spreading her legs for any boy that asks her.'

The boys stepped up readily. Their amusement turning into something darker as they grabbed Sylvia by the ankles and dragged her legs open as she screamed. Even her shrieks weren't enough to drown out Gert's roaring sermon. Every sentence punctuated with another stamp of her foot on the girl's groin. 'Women are unclean creatures. God doesn't love them the way he loves men. He's right not to love them. They're filthy. They're worms grovelling at the feet of men for affection and scraps. So desperate for their attention and their money that they'll do all manner of unholy things to get it. There's none more unholy than a prostitute. A woman who'd sell her most precious innocence to a man for a few measly dollars.'

Gert was beginning to tire. One of her kicks went awry and scraped over the knuckles of one of the boys holding

Sylvia's legs up. He dropped her leg and for one awful moment the girl dangled, kicking, in the other boy's grasp, then he dropped her too and stepped back. Sylvia curled up around the burning ache between her legs and groaned. Gert staggered back and heaved in a few breaths before starting her ranting again.

'The Lord detests whores. And I'm a godly woman so I hate them, too. As all you children of God should. This miserable worm before us has taken money from a man. She has let him touch her down there in her special place. Now she is pregnant. She has ruined her whole life with her lustful, greedy, wicked, filthy ways. She is beneath you all. You should all hate her like I do. Every one of you. If you're good children, godly children, then you'll hate this whore.'

The laughter died away and the room fell into silence. The record had reached its end but nobody moved to change it. The regular thumping sound of the black disk completing another rotation was the only noise in the room apart from the soft sounds of Sylvia's sobbing.

With agonising slowness, Sylvia rolled onto her knees and started to get back onto her feet. Her arms were shaking with the pain, her fingers were leaving indentations in the unfinished plaster. She barely had the strength to stand. It felt like all the blood in her body was rushing down to where Gert had been kicking her and leaving the rest of her numb and useless. She went on groaning when she had the breath, not intentionally, not even consciously. The pain needed to find some way out, and her mouth seemed to be the only option. She wobbled on her feet for a long moment while the other children stared at her, then she lurched in painful half-steps towards the nearest empty chair. Gert got there faster. As Sylvia tried to lower herself gently, Gert jerked the seat away and the girl fell to the floor. She didn't scream at the surprise. After this long living with the Baniszewski children, discovering that her seat had been torn away from under her was practically the normal state of affairs. But when her aching crotch bounced off the bare floorboards it was like someone had shoved a red-hot poker up into her insides. She wailed.

Gert leaned over so far that she nearly toppled, staggering forward to loom so close to Sylvia's face that her ashtray breath ruffled her fringe. 'Whores are unfit for chairs.'

Petty Vengeance

Sylvia was no longer allowed to sit anywhere in the house. Even the pile of dirty laundry that she used as a bed was dispersed by Gert's kicking feet before she was allowed to lie down at night. The few times that Sylvia had tried to sit down without thinking had resulted in another screeching sermon from Gert on her filthiness, the filthiness of women in general, and then moved on to more general musings about the kinds of liquids that might come oozing out of a whore when she sat down. It had made Sylvia nauseated enough to never try sitting in the house again.

When she went to school the day after she had been kicked. She struggled to sit at her desk comfortably. Letting out a little whimper when she sat down and drawing a snigger from her classmate Stephanie Baniszewski. A snigger that she then accompanied with a lewd hand gesture to the girl sitting beside her by way of explanation. Sylvia didn't cry. She'd learned well enough by now that crying did no good. Instead of getting upset, she got angry, and while it wasn't in her power to hurt Gert directly, she could certainly lash out at her lesser tormentors.

During her school days, Gert had never been able to handle the rumours about her, riding on the wave of the ones that she could use, but never really understanding how they spread. Even as an adult she struggled to keep her secrets to herself, misunderstanding human nature so much that she believed the little favours she did in letting the neighbourhood children linger around her house would keep them from talking about the disgusting state it was in, or speculating about her children. In fact, her very deliberate attempts to suppress any information coming out of her home had created a kind of vacuum of information where people would believe almost anything about them, especially if it came from a source close to the family. Like a lodger.

Despite the humiliations that she had endured up until this point, Sylvia was fairly innocent, and even if she had intended on spreading a nasty rumour about someone she probably wouldn't have known where to start—if someone hadn't spent the previous night repeatedly screaming about an apparently evil act. The fact that Sylvia was so innocent just added more credence to the things that she was saying about the Baniszewski girls. After all, how would sweet, innocent

Sylvia Likens even know what prostitution was if she hadn't seen it with her own two eyes? Jenny picked up the story from her at lunchtime, and by the end of the day, the whole school was buzzing with the rumours. Paula and Stephanie Baniszewski had been having sex with boys for money.

The Baniszewski girls never heard a word about it themselves, but they weren't stupid, they knew that something was going on when conversations suddenly dried up the moment that they came into earshot. They might not have had Sylvia's credibility or general likeability, but they did have a well-entrenched support network at the school. Friends soon began to hunt down the source of the rumours, without ever telling Paula or Stephanie what was happening, to spare them the embarrassment. Given that the stories included first-hand descriptions of the interior of the Baniszewski house, including areas that had been off-limits to visitors since Paula fell pregnant, it wasn't difficult to work out where they were coming from. Sibling rivalry wasn't non-existent in the Baniszewski household, but there were limits to how far any one of them might have gone to spite the others, limits that were largely enforced by how much Gert would be willing to tolerate before she'd consider these little betrayals to be giving her a bad name around town. It was obvious to anyone who knew the family that none of them would be spreading this kind of rumour, which left only the Likens girls.

Still, nobody wanted to be the one to tell them. The whole situation was gruesomely awkward to begin with, but when these new rumours intersected with both the events of the previous night and the persistent suspicion that Paula was pregnant, it created the kind of social hornet's nest that nobody wanted to go poking at.

As luck would have it, there was one teenage boy who knew about the situation and who suffered from a complete lack of social awareness and had no sense of self-preservation. Coy Hubbard was fifteen years old and he was in love. Stephanie Baniszewski was the first girl he had ever 'gone steady' with, so he supplemented his lack of real-life experience with movies and a great deal of fantasy. When he heard the rumours about his beloved, he was ready to start punching whoever was spreading them, and it was only the timely intervention of some of Steph's other friends that had prevented him from brawling his way around the entire school that day, redirecting his fury where they thought it belonged.

After classes were over, he headed straight to the Baniszewski house, where Gert greeted him with suspicion. This was a boy of her younger daughter's age, obviously fixated upon her and now lurking around near her bedroom. He wasn't a regular attendee of their open house and he seemed extremely pent up about something. It hadn't been so long ago that Gert could remember being that age, and her first assumption was that he was there for sex, so she tried to drive him off. It was only when he started rambling about 'teaching that bitch a lesson' that Gert actually started listening to him. She fell entirely silent as he explained the rumours that Sylvia and her sister had been spreading, and Gert's expression became more and more blank with every word. Eventually, she brought him into the living room and sat him down with a soda to wait. The two of them lingered in silence until the rest of the family returned home in a noisy rush with the Likens girls trailing along at their heels.

The moment that Sylvia stepped into the room, Coy rushed at her with grim determination. Gert sat back and watched the show. 'Why did you say those things about my girl?'

Sylvia was frozen in indecision. This was a boy from school, where it was safe, but she was in the house, where it wasn't safe. She didn't know whether she should fall silent like she did when she was receiving her abuse from Gert, or if she could talk back. She let out a little strangled noise.

'Why were you saying Stephanie was a slut? Stephanie isn't like that.'

Stephanie barged over. 'What were you saying about me?'

Sylvia's eyes flicked back and forth between them, then locked onto Gert where she was sitting, smiling, across the room from her. 'I didn't... I didn't say...'

'You told people that Steph was screwing guys for money. You told them she was a whore.'

Stephanie shrieked. 'You're the whore. Everyone knows that.'

'Whore,' Coy barked in her face.

'I didn't do anything... I didn't...'

'You know you shouldn't talk about my girl that way. I know judo. I'll mess you up. You say something like that again. There's going to be consequences. You understand me?'

Sylvia was pressed back against the wall. Tears were already pooling in her eyes. She had never expected anything like this. This wasn't how people were supposed to behave.

Gert's smile was slowly forced off her face. 'There'll be no stopping it now. It'll spread all around town. Everyone will hear these lies about my beautiful daughter. Everyone will think that your girlfriend is a whore. You're just going to let her off with a warning? What kind of man are you?"

Coy was already shaking with rage, but at that, his face flushed red and he lashed out. His fist caught Sylvia on the cheek and she let out a yelp, falling to the ground. She was weak from her long bout of malnourishment and even if she weren't, she had never taken a beating before and she didn't know how. Coy grabbed her by the front of her blouse and dragged her back to her feet. Gert called out in a stage whisper to her children. 'This is judo, is it?'

On her feet again, Sylvia swayed for a moment, then her whole world flipped upside down. Coy had grabbed her by the arm and the next thing she knew, she was lying on her back in the middle of the room, gasping for the air he had driven out of her. A fiery stab of pain shot up from her black and blue crotch and the air she was struggling to drag in escaped her in a whine.

The Baniszewski kids all shuffled back in silence. They weren't going to intervene on Sylvia's behalf, not when it was so obvious that Gert wanted this to happen, but they still felt uncomfortable with this stranger in their house doing violence. If it had been one of them it would have been fine, normal even, but for someone who wasn't part of the family to come and beat on Sylvia was like a stranger coming in and washing the dishes. They couldn't object, because they wanted it done, but it was still awkward. Gert met Coy's eyes across the room when he looked at her for approval and she gave a tiny nod before he leapt forward to drag Sylvia onto her feet again. He flipped her again before she'd even pulled in a breath to scream, and this time the floorboards bowed beneath them as he slammed her down and a chair toppled over. Gert frowned. 'You're going to smash up everything messing around like that. Pick her up.'

There was another long pause as everyone waited to see what was going to happen next. Coy wasn't one of her kids or even one of the neighbourhood children who she'd laid claim to. He could refuse her and everything that was happening could stop. He reached down and grabbed the gasping girl by her ponytail, hauling her to her feet. Then he looked askance.

Gert gave another curt nod. 'Door to the basement is in kitchen. Nothing to break down there.'

Sylvia whimpered as he dragged her through the house by her hair, but she understood her place in all this now. She wasn't going to risk enraging Gert by talking or contradicting her. In the end, she still had control over this situation, because she could control herself. This wasn't going to be forever. The boy would throw her around a little bit. She'd get some bruises. It wasn't the end of the world. She'd survived worse than this already. She repeated the same lies to herself over and over and he dragged her down the stairs into the basement. The floor was dirt and there was a single bare lightbulb hanging just low enough that Sylvia had to flinch away so it didn't sear her face. She cast a quick nervous glance back to the stairs. It was all right. Gert hadn't seen that. She was just coming down now. Coy didn't wait for further approval. He flung Sylvia into the wall.

Gert settled herself comfortably on the stairs to watch. Her silent glower the only constant in a world that seemed to be constantly in motion. Sylvia was flipped over and flung around so many times that even when Coy stopped she was still too dizzy to stand on her own. He was red-faced and sweating by the time he stopped. Sylvia had been getting colder and colder with each impact and his hands left slimy trails of sweat over her now. She would have shuddered if she wasn't already constantly shaking. Somewhere in the middle of that tempest of violence, she'd lost track of how many times he'd thrown her. How many times she had bounced off the walls and the floor. She ached all over. She was numb to it but now that she was lying still the pain was starting to creep back in. If this was how it felt now, she dreaded the next few hours and days. The platitudes she'd used upstairs didn't do her much good down here. At least it was over. The boy had his petty revenge. Gert probably felt like she'd been suitably punished. She didn't have to worry about anything but getting through this pain.

Coy staggered, half exhausted, towards the stairs, and he was almost past Gert when her hand wrapped around his thigh and he froze. The old woman looked flushed, he could hear her panting echoing back across the cellar as if she'd been the one throwing the girl around. 'You're good at that judo, but you could be better.'

'I'm the best in my class.'

She squeezed at the muscles of his thigh approvingly. 'Maybe you are, but wouldn't it help to be able to practice a little more? You know you can come back down here any time you want to work up a sweat.'

The perplexed expression on his face was starting to irritate Gert. 'If you want to practice your judo. You come back here and try it out on her some more. She deserves it. She deserves worse. Telling them lies about your girl. About my baby girl. It wasn't right.'

Coy lingered for another moment before grunting 'all right' and striding off up the stairs.

Gert stayed right where she was, sitting on the steps and watching Sylvia vibrating helplessly on the floor. She wet her lips. 'You just stay there tonight. None of my food is going to be passing those nasty lying lips of yours.'

She hauled herself upright and then flicked off the light. Leaving Sylvia alone in the cold darkness, waiting for the pain to come in like the tide.

Turning Inward

Sylvia tried to return to a normal life after her first night in the basement, but she was so bruised and battered that she was barely able to move when she woke up swollen and stiff in the morning. Her sister and the other children were already gone by the time she had crawled to the top of the stairs. Gert was waiting for her, perched on the one kitchen chair that was still intact. 'Everyone might have heard the lies you told about my daughter, but you can be damned sure that everyone knows you for a liar now. I don't need to punish you. You've brought enough misery down on yourself. Don't ever let me catch you with my daughter's names in your mouth again, whore.'

After the weekend, Sylvia returned to school, supposedly recovered from her bout of 'flu'. The bruises protruding beyond her deliberately prudish clothes had faded to yellow, and the Baniszewski girls were generous about sharing their makeup, at least until the yellowing had faded enough that it could just be passed off as bad skin. Sylvia completely withdrew from the Baniszewskis at school. She couldn't risk anything that she said or did trickling back to Gert, or for Coy to get mad at her again. It was clear that the protections any child enjoyed had been withdrawn from her, that anyone would be allowed to hurt her if she had angered Gert. It drove any possibility that Gert was just overzealous in her disciplinary habits out of the window. Despite the beating she had taken, and Gert's threats the next day, Sylvia still didn't feel like the axe had fallen on her yet. Doom followed the girl.

Still, life wasn't entirely terrible. When she was at school there were several friends she could rely on for distraction from her nightmarish home life. Anna Sisco was the closest friend she'd managed to make outside of her sister. She was thirteen years old, and if the Likens girls were sheltered compared to the more worldly Baniszewskis, they were nothing compared to Anna. She genuinely couldn't understand why she was never invited back to Sylvia's house, or why Sylvia wouldn't come back to hers and risk questioning about where she had been. There was a constant fear about bringing someone home to Gert. It was bad enough that Sylvia and Jenny were in the old woman's power. She didn't want to deliver someone else into the hag's clutches if she could avoid it. Worse yet, she had no idea how little Anna would respond to the treatment that she received in the Baniszewski house. If she tried to stand up for Sylvia or tried to report Gert, Sylvia had no idea what fresh hell would be unleashed.

Adding to the swirling chaos that Anna might have walked into in the Baniszewski house were the regular visits from Coy. He never abused Sylvia as much as he had the first night when he was in a rage, but Gert would still send him down into the basement with her, where Sylvia was expected to submit to his whims. Not that those whims ever seemed to extend beyond throwing her around. She didn't know how she could explain her ready acceptance to Anna in terms that would make sense to a sane person. She could barely rationalise it herself.

Eventually, Sylvia gave in to Anna's badgering and she brought her home on a weeknight when the swarms of teenagers that lingered around the house were likely to be thinner than usual. She thought that if she could show the younger girl the state of the house then she might be embarrassed enough on Sylvia's behalf that she wouldn't press the issue further. The record player was silent when they came in, which was a good sign. Gert was sitting in the living room, patiently waiting for some entertainment. Which was not a good sign. It was not a good sign at all. She caught Sylvia's eye and there was a glimmer of a wicked smile on her face for only a moment before she switched to her charming neighbourhood mother routine. 'What's this? A friend of our Sylvie? I'm so glad to finally meet you.'

Sylvia froze. She had only one moment to try and get control of this situation before Gert rolled right over her, the way that she always did, smothering her with her skewed version of reality until there was nothing that she could do except accept it. She opened her mouth, but it was already too late. Gert patted the seat beside her, all smiles and matronly approval. 'Won't you come take a seat. Sylvia hasn't told us a thing about you and we're all so curious. What's your name, girl? Come on now, don't be shy. Sit yourself down.' She turned to Sylvia with that same placid smile. 'Why don't you go and fetch your friend a soda?'

With feet that felt like lead, Sylvia trudged through to the kitchen and fetched the bottles. She had no idea what she was going to be walking back into. She didn't even have time to speak before Anna's fist caught her in the cheek. She staggered back into the hallway, completely aghast. Anna rushed at her again, swinging her fists wildly, barely connecting at the best of times and sobbing all the while. Eventually, Sylvia heard her shrill cries underneath the grunts of exertion. 'How dare you? How dare you tell people those things about my mother? You... you're a nasty liar. I'm going to tell everyone what a... I thought you were my friend!'

She pushed past Sylvia and rushed out into the street, tears streaming down her face. Sylvia was so shocked she didn't even try to follow her. Gert shook her head sadly. 'You really must stop telling lies, Sylvie. Otherwise, everyone is going to end up hating you. You wouldn't want that, would you? Wouldn't want the whole world to know that you are a vicious, lying little whore.'

Sylvia crossed the distance between them in a few strides and for one moment as she loomed over the haggard old woman, Gert's bottomless pit of confidence seemed to betray her. She almost flinched. It was enough to snap the girl out of it. She wasn't like the Baniszewskis. She wasn't a monster. She couldn't hurt people just for being cruel. She was better than that. She was better than Gert. She let some tiny part of that superiority show in her polite smile. 'Here is your soda. Mom.'

With the loss of Anna and the consequent rumours that began to spread about her untrustworthiness, Sylvia became completely isolated at school. Some small part of the rumours must have spread out into the adults of the community too, because before long teachers who would gladly cut her slack on account of her difficult circumstances turned cold to her. They started to treat the girl with suspicion in everything that she said and did. There were eyes on her constantly. It was like Gert had suddenly extended her reach, remaking the world in her image all over again. A world in which there was only one villain, Sylvia Likens.

Gert was unsatisfied with the way that her last torture had gone. She hadn't liked the spark of defiance that the whore had in her eyes, and that smug smile needed to be wiped off her face. She needed to know her place, looking down on Gert like she was any better than her. Gert had never spread her legs for money. She wasn't a whore. She'd been with her husbands, all legal and fair like the Lord wanted, and they might have bought her things and paid the bills, but that was how it was meant to be. Sylvia was the whore, and whores belonged on their knees. When Sylvia got home from the church social, where she had very carefully avoided eating much of anything despite the protests from her aching stomach, the house was packed with teenagers again. Stephanie hadn't bothered to come along, banking on the new clout that bringing Coy into the fold had bought her with Gert to excuse her from having to make nice with Reverend Julian for a little while. Instead, she had made the house into her own private party, inviting all of the kids from her year at school, the same teenagers who now looked at Sylvia with contempt and even outright hatred. Out of all the kids in the room, only one of them seemed furious enough to actually do something about it.

Judy Duke loomed over Sylvia, a head taller and almost double her weight after the recent bout of near starvation. She slapped Sylvia in the face then sneered as blood trickled out from between the smaller girl's lips. 'Why are you telling people my mom is a hooker?'

Sylvia glanced at Gert and sighed. How many times was this same script going to be played out? 'I don't even know your mom, Judy. I barely even know you. So why would I say something like that?'

Another slap. Softer but still stinging. 'I don't know why a lying freak like you says horrible things about other people. Maybe you're just horrible.'

'I didn't say anything about your mom, Judy. Somebody is telling you that so you'll fight with me.'

There was a long moment of silence before Gert's soft hiss cut through. 'Lies. Always more lies with this one.'

Judy kicked Sylvia in the shins with as much rage as she could muster, but there was doubt on her face, Sylvia could see it. They might have all been caught up in the maelstrom of chaos and wickedness that Gert sowed, but her pawns were still people. A couple of kicks later, it became clear that Sylvia wasn't going to fight back and Judy stormed out of the house, confusion still written all over her face. Gert was fuming. This wasn't what she had wanted at all. It wasn't good enough. She wasn't going to stand for it. She barked, 'Hit her.'

The music went on playing, a woman's voice crooning out, 'What the world needs now is love, sweet love,' obscene in the tense silence.

Stephanie squirmed. 'Who?'

Gert's eyes bulged. 'Hit the whore!'

Stephanie leaned away from her mother as the old woman vibrated with rage. 'No, mom. Who are you talking to? Who do you want to hit her?'

Gert cast her gaze around the room until they locked onto someone right beside Sylvia. With a dull sense of dread, Sylvia turned around to meet her sister's eyes. Jenny was already shaking her head frantically. Gert growled. 'Hit her. Hit the whore. Box her ears. I'll not have lying whores walking around unpunished. Hit her.'

Coy leaned over, 'I'll do it.'

'No. Her,' Gert snarled. 'She needs to be the one to do it. She needs to prove that she isn't on the whore's side in all this. That she'll stand by her family, not this degenerate.'

Jenny was shaking, tears already pricking the corners of her eyes. 'I... I won't.'

Sylvia shook her head. 'Do it.'

'I can't,' Jenny wailed. 'She's my sister. I can't.'

Gert lunged up out of her chair and crossed the room so fast that it was hard to believe. She slapped Jenny across the face. 'You do it or you get it instead. Hit her or I'll send you and Coy down to the basement for him to practice. Do it or you'll be eating nothing for the rest of the week. Do it. Hit the whore.'

Jenny was still shaking her head, even as Sylvia whimpered. 'For God's sake, just do it.'

Gert hit the girl. She slapped her so hard that Jenny's weak legs couldn't even support her. She cast around and snarled, 'Don't you take the Lord's name in vain. You filth. You aren't fit to speak his name.'

'Jenny, please. Just do it.'

Sobbing, the girl made a fist and lunged out. It caught Sylvia by surprise. She staggered back a step with a yelp of pain. This close, she could see Gert's eyes light up. She could hear her ragged breathing getting faster. The woman's face was a carefully tamed mask of misery, but there were little things like the flush spreading on her cheeks that told another story. She was enjoying this. Jenny hit her again with a sob. She beat Sylvia in the face until her knuckles were red and bruising before the hag dragged her off with a mock scolding. With her obligations as the evening's entertainment fulfilled, Sylvia stalked off to her room without another word. Gert's eyes bored into the back of her head every step of the way.

A Cure for Sticky Fingers

Sylvia showed up to school bruised and battered more and more frequently. Coy seemed to be enjoying having free range to toss her around, and his violence was beginning to escalate beyond practicing his judo into closed-fist beatings and a few brief bouts where he ground Sylvia against a wall with his body and wrapped his fingers around her neck. All of his dark fantasies could be fulfilled down in the dim lit basement, if he had the courage to go through with them. Until he got the guts to go further, he kept on escalating his beatings. After all, it wasn't like anyone cared what happened to Sylvia.

Despite all of this, life continued to move on around the Baniszewski house. Summer started to ease into autumn and fitness classes at the school remained outside. The shorts and shirt that her parents had provided were no longer enough protection against the elements, so Sylvia had to swallow the tattered remains of her pride and ask Gert to buy her a tracksuit. She thought that she'd caught the old woman in a good mood, but as it turned out, Gert didn't have good moods when it came to Sylvia. 'Wouldn't a whore do better if she didn't cover up?'

She bit back her denial. There was no point arguing. 'The school says it is the uniform. I've got to wear one.'

'Doesn't matter to me one way or the other.' Gert flicked ash onto the floor. 'There's no money for new clothes right now. Especially for the likes of you.'

'But I need it.' There was an edge of whining to Sylvia's voice that grated on Gert's nerves.

'And I don't give a damn what you need.'

At school before the next session of jogging around the field, Sylvia panicked. If she went out without a sweat suit, then the school would call Gert. They might even visit the house. If Sylvia brought that kind of attention down on the Baniszewski house, then she would be signing her own death warrant. Gert would blame her for everything and go berserk. She couldn't risk that. With a heavy heart, she slunk into the changing rooms before the bell rang and stole a tracksuit from one of the lockers. She didn't even know whose clothes she was taking but she hoped against hope that they could afford to replace them easily. Not that there was anyone at the school as bad off as her and her sister. She hid in the bathroom until everyone else was dressed then went out jogging onto the field with the rest of her class. Whoever she had stolen from must have had a spare kit because she didn't see anyone in their summer gear. She let out a little sigh of relief and tried to ignore the niggling guilt that raced after her when she broke into a run. She supposed that she should have been thrilled to get away with it with nobody being hurt, but she felt sick.

Gert spotted the new tracksuit when Sylvia tried to wash it. The old woman seemed completely obtuse most of the time. Barely literate as far as Sylvia could tell. Yet somehow when it came to things like this she was eerily astute. 'Where did you get that from?'

Sylvia froze on the spot. She couldn't help it. Every time Gert spoke to her it was like nails on a chalkboard in her head. There was no point in arguing or resisting. Whatever Gert decided to bellow would become the truth anyway. Gert snatched the clothes from her hands and stared at them long and hard. 'Stole it did you? I won't have thieves in my house. I won't stand for it.'

Sylvia kept her mouth clamped shut. The truth was that she had stolen it, but she hadn't really expected Gert to care. There was a steady supply of cigarettes and soda coming into the house each day, both in the hands of the Baniszewski kids and the visiting teenagers, and Sylvia knew for a fact that there was no money for them to buy them with. Every cigarette that Gert smoked had been stolen, but there she was puffing away on one and damning Sylvia for doing what she needed to survive. It wasn't fair. It just wasn't fair. Sylvia expected the slap. She was braced for it. She gave Gert nothing. No yelp. No flinch.

Gert hit her again, harder. There was surprising strength in the woman's wiry arms, a reminder that while she might have looked elderly and decrepit she wasn't that much older than Sylvia's real mother. When that still wasn't enough, Gert grabbed Sylvia by the hair and threw her down onto the filthy kitchen floor. There were still yellow stains here and there. A reminder of the last time they had been together in the kitchen like this that made Sylvia's stomach start to churn. Gert kicked her and took a long draw on her cigarette. A halo of blue smoke drifting around her as she hissed. 'Did you steal it, or did you buy it? Did you buy it with your whoring money?'

The next kick was to a familiar place. The bruises from the last time had finally faded but each time Gert's heel collided with Sylvia's crotch it set her whole pelvis alight with searing pain again. She cried out. She couldn't help it. Gert smirked. 'You like that whore? Can you even feel it after all the men that have used you? This is just another day for you, isn't it? Just another day lying on your back. Spreading your legs for whoever wants you. Is this how you got clothes money? When my babies have to wear hand-me-downs because you were too stupid to keep your legs shut when some man wanted you?'

Sylvia tried to crabwalk away, to get out of reach, but Gert pursued her. Eyes glazed. Heel grinding down into Sylvia's most tender parts at every opportunity. 'How many men did you fuck for those clothes? How many times did they squirt their poison inside you? You could have had a life. You could have been happy. But now you're nothing but a stupid, worthless whore. That's all you'll ever be now. Whore. Whore!'

Sylvia was screaming, still trying to crawl away. She didn't want to defy Gert but the pain, now that it was back, seemed even worse than the first time. It was like someone had shoved a red-hot poker inside her. Searing pain radiated up her body and her legs were limp and numb. Gert's cigarette tumbled out of her mouth as she bellowed, 'Whore! Whore!' over and over. It landed on Sylvia and she yelped in surprise. Suddenly, Gert was still and silent. When she spoke again, her voice was hoarse. 'You stole it. You... you're a thief. You need to be punished like a thief.'

She stumbled back across the room and lit another cigarette. Sylvia curled up in a ball around the boiling knot of pain inside her. Shaking and shivering. Trying to stay silent. Hoping against all evidence that Gert would just forget about her.

When she felt Gert's leathery hands taking hold of hers ever so gently and drawing them away from her body, she actually believed that it was over. That Gert felt like discipline had been dispensed. When her clenched fingers were uncurled with a firm but gentle grip, it was almost a comfort. The only time that anyone had touched her without the intent to cause pain in so long that she started sobbing. She could feel Gert's breath ghosting over the palm of her hand. 'Only one cure for thieves.'

There was no pain quite like a burn. It was instantly recognisable even though Sylvia had only ever touched the stove once as a little girl, so long ago that the actual event had long since fled her memory. She yelped and tried to pull her hand away, but Gert's grip on her was like steel. She entangled their fingers and held the weakened girl still without even a hint of strain. She moved the cigarette along to the next finger in line and then pressed down. The pain was immediate. Intense. It made her forget all about her battered crotch. She wailed and then sobbed as the cigarette was pulled away and then puffed a few times to get it hot again. Sylvia felt like she was going to go mad from the pain and that had only been two fingers. She still had eight left to go. When she tried to struggle away Gert sat on her, pinned her arm between clammy thighs and let out a high-pitched giggle. 'This is what thieves deserve. This is all you deserve.'

The Cola Bottle

If Sylvia had thought that her punishment was over just because every one of her fingers had been seared and she had passed out from the pain, she was sorely mistaken. Pain was only part of the lesson. There had to be humiliation, too. In the living room, in full view of all the neighbourhood boys, her skirts were lifted up and her panties were pulled down. Gert beat her with a belt until there were welts across her buttocks and thighs, then she dropped her onto the filthy ground. The children had all been informed of her indiscretion in one of Gert's sermons before the beating began, but now the time had arrived for them to participate in the punishment. Gert quietly encouraged them to burn the girl as a regular reminder that stealing was wrong. One by one, the children, some as young as twelve, stepped forward to put their cigarette out on Sylvia's bare flesh. She wailed each time, but that only served as encouragement for the more sadistic boys. Coy put his cigarette out on her thigh, as close as he could get to her vagina without accusations of infidelity from Stephanie.

From that day forward, Sylvia became a living ashtray for the Baniszewski house. Each burn was meant to serve as a reminder that she should not steal. Instead, they taught her an entirely different lesson. With no nutrition and almost no sleep due to her constant fear, Sylvia's body had stopped healing. The burns on her fingertips were still there, barely changed, a week after her punishment. Coy had come back for another session the day after he had burned her and while he was getting braver, he still didn't do much more than smack her around. The bruises, when they came up, were a dull dirty brown and they didn't fade. It was like her whole body was slowing down. She had been hungry for so long that she'd forgotten what it felt like to be any other way. It had become background noise to the more alarming pains that had started to develop across her body. Particularly in her pelvis. Her periods had stopped shortly after she arrived in the Baniszewski house, whether due to stress or starvation. Gert hadn't noticed yet, but when she did, it was certain to be used as more evidence that she was pregnant, despite never having been near enough to a boy who wasn't actively maiming her in the last few months. It became clear to Sylvia that she couldn't just keep on hoping and waiting for her situation to resolve itself. The burns on her fingers were a testament to that. Her body was shutting down. She was going to die if she didn't take action.

With the whole town convinced that she was a liar, she didn't have anyone to reach out to for help, so she returned to her original plan to deal with her starvation. She collected as many soda bottles as she could find around the house, then roamed the streets gathering more from the trash to trade in for pocket money. She knew that there were risks. Not just the very real risks of being a teenage girl roaming the street of Indianapolis at night, but the far more terrifying prospect that Gert would realise she was missing, but she had run out of other options. She needed to eat.

Her first night out of the house was a roaring success. She managed to scrape together enough money to buy almost a meal's worth of food, which she sat on a bench and ate before she headed home. She would have liked to have shared with her sister, but there was no guarantee that anything she brought with her wouldn't be confiscated. It would certainly have been used as evidence against her in the latest of Gert's witch hunts. With her stomach full for the first time in months, Sylvia made her way home and tried to sneak through to her room unnoticed in all of the usual evening hubbub. Gert didn't seem to be in the midst of the laughter and jeering tonight. For a moment Sylvia thought that she had gotten lucky for once, that the old woman had gone to bed early. The moment she stepped into her room she realised that luck was never on her side. Gert was there. Waiting for her.

She didn't even try to fight as Gert dragged her through to the living room. She tried to go away inside her head. None of this mattered. She had eaten. She was going to get her strength back. She was going to walk away from all of this. All of this was temporary. The bruises would fade. The shame, the humiliation, it would all pass. She was stronger than this. Gert tossed her into the room and every eye was turned her way. Sylvia should have been past embarrassment by now, but she still flushed as all eyes turned her way. Old habits die hard. Her shame wasn't helped by Gert's bellowing. 'Look what the cat dragged in. Our very own lady of the night has finally finished walking the streets.'

Sylvia glanced around nervously. A few of the neighbourhood kids were smoking. This could get very painful, very quickly, if she wasn't careful. 'What's the matter, whore? You're suddenly shy now? You spent all night parading your body around for men. Stripping off your clothes. Spreading your legs for them. Now you're blushing?'

Gert was right behind her. She could feel the weight of the monster's presence against her back. She leaned in close enough for her tarry breath to tickle Sylvia's ear. 'Are you too good for these boys? Is that it? You'll go whoring around all your fancy men, but these good boys here, you think you're better than them?'

Sylvia's eyes were still darting around the room. There were hardly any girls here at all tonight, and while she didn't think Gert's nonsense was really going to make these boys angry, everything was so confusing right now that they could all attack her at a moment's notice. That was the most frightening thing about what Gert had done. She'd stripped all of the rules away so that she could put hers in their place, but there were all these huge grey areas where anything could happen. Places where Gert hadn't made a decision yet. The old woman had drifted away from her now to go lean against the doorway, trapping her in the room. 'Go on then, whore. Give the boys a show. I know you want to. They know you want to. Everyone knows you're a whore. So do it.'

Sylvia had already started shaking and her voice cracked as she asked, 'Do what?'

'Strip for them, whore.'

Her hands moved with a will of their own. Her body betraying her. A month ago, Sylvia would have died rather than take her clothes off in front of a room full of boys, but now her pride and her shame had been ground down by terror. She slipped her skirt down her legs. Then unbuttoned her blouse and dropped it on top of the pile. She slipped off her shoes and kicked them forward too. She was trying not to look at the boys. She didn't know what she might see there and, if her humiliation had provoked lust, she didn't know if she could stomach it. She wasn't sure if she could manage pity either. It was safer to keep her eyes locked on the dust-crusted floorboards. 'And the rest. Whores aren't fit for clothes.'

Sylvia closed her eyes. She undid her bra and dropped it to the floor. She hooked her thumbs in her underwear and jerked them down. She was crying. It wasn't intentional. If it had been up to her, she would have given Gert nothing—this was just another way that her body was betraying her. The shaking legs. Her nipples tightening in the cold air. The hysterical sobbing that she was only barely able to hold back by keeping her eyes scrunched shut as tightly as she could. Pretending that she was all alone.

Gert growled. 'There's a good whore. Now give them a show. Let them see what you do for your money, whore.'

Sylvia didn't know what she was being asked to do. She stood there frozen. Resisting the urge to cover herself or run from the room because she didn't want to feel the sting of Gert's belt again. Being beaten while she was naked would have been more than she could stand. She felt something nudge against her hand, and despite desperately wanting to keep her eyes shut and the tide of tears held back, she couldn't help but look down. Gert was trying to put an empty glass cola bottle in her hand. Sylvia just stared at it. Eventually, with a few more nudges she took it, but it still made no sense. Why was Gert giving her a bottle? Was she admitting that she knew what Sylvia had really been doing all night? Was her punishment finally over? 'Put on a show. Like you do when you're whoring. Shove it inside.'

Nothing she was saying made any sense. Sylvia just stared at her blankly until Gert growled and seized her by the wrist, guiding the bottle down until it nudged against her bruised vagina. No. She couldn't possibly want that. Gert growled. 'Do it, you whore. Do it.'

The chant got picked up. The boy's usual pubescent voices seemed deeper than usual. Some animal part of them was growling out. 'Do it. Do it. Do it.'

Sylvia looked up and there was a dreadful hunger on their faces. Even though some of the boys were flushed red and looking ashamed of themselves, they still weren't looking away. Every eye in the room was on Sylvia, on that most secret and well-hidden part of Sylvia that was now on display for the world to see. She swallowed back the bile that was rushing up her throat and pressed the open neck of the bottle inside. It was cold, even compared to the chill of the room and her hands were shaking so badly that she almost dropped it. She wondered what would happen if she did drop it. Would Gert go and fetch another? Would she make her use the broken glass in the same way? She tightened her grip on the textured glass and shoved it a little further in. It was starting to hurt now as the neck got wider and the end went deeper. Sylvia was doing everything that she could to keep her hard-earned meal down, but it was a losing battle. She needed to hurry. If she could just get it done then she could sneak away. She could lie down in her room and go to sleep and pretend that none of this had ever happened. A little whimper escaped her as she shoved the bottle deeper inside and the boys, they leaned forward, practically salivating. Gert was losing patience. 'You keep all the men waiting this long? Hurry up.'

Sylvia tried to push on past the pain, but it was like the bottle had hit some sort of barrier inside her and couldn't go any further. Gert growled. 'I said hurry up.'

The old woman's hand darted out and she slapped the flat bottom of the bottle as hard as she could. Half the length of it vanished inside of Sylvia. Then the pain came. She fell to the floor, screaming so loud that it startled even Gert. Blood trickled down the glass to pool on the floor between Sylvia's knees.

Gert stood over her and scoffed. 'I'm sure you've taken bigger than that, whore. Now fuck yourself with it.'

Sylvia whimpered and tried to pull the bottle out, but even that slight motion had her screaming again. Something was wrong. Something was really wrong. It felt like something inside of her had torn. She shook and she wept. Her shaking hands pawed uselessly at the slippery, bloody glass. Trying desperately to pull it out. Tears were pouring down her face now, any attempt at stoicism lost in the agony of the moment. 'Please. Help me. Oh God. Help.'

Gert rolled her eyes in disgust. 'None of us want to catch your whore diseases. Touching your filthy slit. Pull it out.'

'I... I c-can't.' Sylvia sobbed.

Gert grabbed the bottle, drawing another shriek out of Sylvia. 'Ridiculous girl.'

She tore it out of Sylvia and another shrill wail came with it. There was a half inch of blood and other murky fluids pooled inside the bottle when Gert held it up to the light. That made her stop for a moment. When she turned back to Sylvia, the girl had passed out. With exaggerated disgust, Stephanie and Paula dragged her off to bed. The cola bottle was tossed out with the rest of the trash and forgotten about promptly.

The Basement

The next morning, Sylvia woke up in a puddle of her own blood-tinged urine. It had chilled through the night without waking her. The pain from her injuries was bad enough that she couldn't even stand, but she tried to bundle up the dirty clothes that she had wet and crawl through to wash them before Gert could realise. Of course, the old woman caught her in the act again. She looked down at the filthy, naked and bloodstained girl and sighed. 'You just aren't fit to live with humans anymore. Can't even keep yourself from pissing all over. You're like a dog. You're worse than a dog. At least a dog can be trained. I wish we'd got a dog rather than you and your half-wit sister.'

Sylvia lay on the floor of the kitchen and wept until Gert started to kick her. 'Down you go. Down into your kennel.

You're not fit for chairs, you're not fit for clothes and now you're not fit for beds.'

Sylvia sobbed, 'Please. Please help me. I need a doctor. I need help.'

Gert's eyes narrowed. 'Do you have doctor money? Because I don't.'

She took a hold of Sylvia's hair and dragged her, wailing, across the floor to the basement door, then she kicked her inside. Every time that Sylvia managed to halt her tumble into the darkness, Gert would give her another boot in the ribs. She ended up down on the dirt floor of the basement again, weeping and aching like the first time that Coy had his way with her. Without clothes, it didn't take long for the cold to start seeping up from the ground into her body, but she welcomed it. If she was numb then maybe the terrible pain inside her might ease.

That night, Gert came down to study her. She had wet herself again during her fruitless attempts to find sleep. Her injuries had rendered her incontinent. Gert tutted at her. 'Filthy. Absolutely filthy. You'll have to stay down here, dirty girl. We'll have to scrub you down, too. You foul thing.'

Sylvia croaked. 'Please. I need help.'

Gert huffed. 'I'll need help. You've been stuffing your face for so long it'll be a wonder if me or the girls can lift you.'

She gathered up the most useful boys she could find upstairs. Coy, her son John, and another boy from the neighbourhood, Ricky Hobbs, who she had been keeping an eye on for quite some time. Between the three of them, the boys managed to carry the limp Sylvia upstairs and into the bathroom where Gert and Paula were waiting. There was one bath in the house, a claw-footed thing that had to be filled up with hot water boiled on top of the stove. Steam was rising up off the water despite the relative warmth of the room. Without thinking, Ricky dipped his finger in to check the temperature, then let out a yelp. It was scalding hot. Gert nodded to them. 'Dunk her in then.'

Ricky was holding onto Sylvia's legs, the smelliest job handed off to the youngest one. While the other boys made to throw her in, he pulled her back. 'Hang on now, that water will burn her. That's hot as a kettle.'

Paula, Coy and John all glanced nervously at each other, but Gert just laughed. 'Let me just talk with my new assistant here. You boys give her a wash. Paula, you scrub her with that salt when they're done.'

Ricky shook his head. 'This ain't right.'

'No it most certainly is not. Come on now. Let me explain some things to you.' Gert reached out and took his hand, leading him out of the room. He flinched when he heard Sylvia screaming, and he looked like he might run back for a moment, but Gert tightened her grip on his hand and led him through to the boy's bedroom. The only one in the house that still had a door.

She looked him up and down and pushed him onto the bed. 'How old are you now, Ricky?'

He glanced nervously from Gert to the door. He could still hear the sloshing water, but the screams seemed to have stopped. 'I – I'm fourteen, Mrs Wright. Fifteen in a few months.'

She smiled at him. Her teeth seemed longer than normal. Like her gums had crept back from them, or like they were growing out longer so she could take a bite out of him. He shivered. 'Fourteen years old. I never would have guessed. You look so mature.'

He wasn't immune to flattery. A little smile played over his lips. 'Thank you, Mrs Wright.'

'Please. Call me Gertie.'

'G – Gertie. That water. It was much too...'

'You have a girlfriend yet, Ricky? Handsome boy like you, must be beating them off with a stick.'

'No, Mrs ... um... Gertie. No, I don't.'

'Girls your age, hardly worth the time are they? No titties to speak of. Too scared to even touch a boy down there. You're probably just waiting for the right girl to come along, aren't you? The kind of girl that will treat you the way you deserve to be treated.'

She came closer and closer with every word. So close that he could smell the nicotine clinging to her clothes. He leaned back so that she couldn't plant a kiss on him, because that was what it looked like she was going to do, but she had another destination in mind for her lips. She slipped down onto her knees in front of him and unbuttoned his cords with deft fingers. She licked her lips as she looked up at him. 'I need an assistant, Ricky. Somebody to help me deal with that monster in the basement. Someone to help out with the lifting and carrying. I don't have any money to pay you with, but... I can pay you in other ways.'

He shuddered as her hands tightened on his thighs and she leaned closer. She'd done this plenty of times before to get her way, even when there was far less on the line than keeping a little squealer from going running and telling everyone her business. Men were easy to control if you knew where to apply the right pressure.

Three minutes later they came out of the bedroom. Gert clearing her throat and Ricky practically bouncing up and down with excitement. In the bathroom, Sylvia was letting out groans of pain as salt was scraped over her tender red flesh, but Ricky had mysteriously become oblivious to them. He hoisted the girl up into his arms all by himself and carried her down to the basement without faltering, except for a very brief pause to smirk when Gert commented on how strong he was. At the bottom of the stairs, he let Sylvia drop without a second thought. She let out a little cry of pain when she hit the ground, but it was so minor compared to all of her other suffering that it was more of an exhalation than a scream.

Ricky didn't hear it anyway. He was already bounding back up the stairs to the daylight with a grin on his face.

The cleaning regimen continued over the following weeks. Once the initial pain of her internal injuries had passed, Gert had Coy and Ricky bind her hands and feet before carrying her up to the bath. Some days she wouldn't be cleaned at all. Just left alone down in the basement with only the smell of her own excrement for company. Other times, Gert would drag her up and scrub her two or three times over the course of the day. Food was even rarer for Sylvia now that she had been sent to the basement. Gert would bring her down a bowl of soup when she had made a pot, but she refused to give the girl cutlery. Sylvia was an animal, so she had to eat like an animal, trying to scoop the watery broth into her mouth with her bare hands. The only other time that she was allowed to eat was when Gert and the twelve-year-old John Junior came down to clean up the basement. They would scoop up her faeces with a gardening trowel, then Gert would pin Sylvia's jaw open while John poured her own excrement down her throat. When the smell of ammonia started to waft up into the kitchen, Gert threw a few buckets of water on the floor and gave Sylvia an old coffee tin to use as a toilet. Once a day, Gert and Ricky would come down into the basement and force her to drink its contents. The worst part was, those moments of agony in the bath, or humiliation and disgust in the basement, were the highlights of Sylvia's day. The only moments when she was allowed the simple luxury of light.

Missed Opportunities

The treatment of the Likens girls hadn't gone completely unnoticed by the people who had crossed their paths. Judy Duke, who had been goaded into fighting with Sylvia one night by Gert's lies, returned home confused and distraught. She had approached her mother and told her, 'They were beating and kicking Sylvia,' being careful to exclude herself from the guilty parties. Her mother seemed entirely unconcerned, having heard tales about the Likens girls. Their parents were carnies. It was hardly a surprise that they were nasty little liars, turning tricks. She took her daughter by the hand and explained to her that not every girl was as good and well behaved as her, and when a bad girl did a bad thing, sometimes the only punishment that she would understand was violence. Hearing that from her own mother was enough to calm Judy's confusion, but she remained withdrawn from the Baniszewskis' social circle from that point forward.

Not long after the Likens girls were "adopted" into the Baniszewski household, Gert got some new neighbours. The Vermillions purchased the house next to Gert's. The middle-aged professional couple of Raymond and Phyllis Vermillion saw how many children that Gert had under her roof and suspected she would make the ideal babysitter for their own children. Judging the state of her property, they also considered it an act of charity to pay her for that service. Still, they weren't even close to being as negligent as the Likens. Before even broaching the subject of babysitting, they invited the Baniszewski family over for a barbecue to get to know their new neighbours. Gert seemed to bring the whole neighbourhood's worth of teenagers and children with her and the whole event soon became rowdy. Even so, the Vermillions were delighted at the playful atmosphere. At least until they caught sight of one gaunt girl with two black eyes.

Phyllis caught Paula Baniszewski and asked her what had happened to the girl, only to be horrified when Paula proudly announced that she had been the one to give Sylvia the beating. She then vanished into the kitchen and returned with a mug full of boiling water, which she flung into Sylvia's face as Gert nodded approvingly. Needless to say, the Vermillions found a different babysitter.

Despite that, they made no attempt to contact the authorities about Sylvia's treatment. Everyone else in the neighbourhood treated the events that they'd witnessed as completely normal, and that normalised the violence for the Vermillions, too. Even when Phyllis stopped in at the Baniszewski house to borrow a tool for the garden and saw Paula beating Sylvia in the face with a belt until her lip split.

Shortly after Sylvia was condemned to the basement, another opportunity for rescue arose. Reverend Julian had an ongoing program that he had set up to visit his parishioners in their homes in an attempt to make himself seem more accessible. He sat with Gert in the kitchen, mere feet away from the door to the basement, drinking coffee and swallowing down her lies just as readily. 'That Likens girl. That Sylvie. She's been a terrible burden to me, Reverend. It pains me to admit it, but she has been such a blight on this family that it is a wonder I've held things together. If I'd known what she was on that first day when she forced her way inside my home I can tell you that I would have driven her right back out. She is a prostitute. The lowest of the low. The most unholy... not just that, she isn't just soiling herself, she is ruining good mens' lives, too. She services married men, Reverend. Then she comes back here gloating about it. She's pregnant you know. Got knocked up by one of the married men she lay down with.'

Paula wandered into the room in the middle of their conversation. Her stomach was already starting to swell with the baby she was carrying. She was several months along now, just starting to show but not enough that Gert had started dressing her up in baggy clothes. The reverend tried not to stare but Gert had a spark of fury in her eyes when he turned back to her. 'The nasty little liar has been going around trying to blame all her sins—all her crimes—on my sweet Paula. Saying that she is pregnant! It is ridiculous. My Paula is a virgin. As pure as they come. It is despicable the way that Sylvie has treated her. After she invited her into her own home, too.'

The reverend reached out to both of the women and took their hands. 'Let us pray for her.'

It only took a moment before their silent contemplation was interrupted by Paula blurting out. 'I've got hate in my heart for her.'

Gert silenced her with a pointed stare. 'You've got love in your heart for her is what you mean to say. Even though you should hate her for all the ways she's wronged you.'

Paula mumbled. 'Yeah. I don't hate her.'

The reverend scheduled another visit to discuss the troubles that the family had been having, walked out of the house and promptly forgot about it all.

Out of all the people in the world, there was only one that the Likens girls could reach out to. Their previous attempts to contact their parents had been thwarted by their constantly shifting address, information that only Gert was privy to. They had no aunts or uncles, and while they had a grandmother, she was ailing, impoverished and already taking care of Jenny's twin brother Benny. There was only one other family member who they had a hope of contacting. Their sister Diana.

When Sylvia was first condemned to the basement, Jenny sent a detailed letter explaining all of the torture that they had been experiencing at the hands of the Baniszewski family. A full accounting of it from start to finish. She begged her sister to send the police to the house to rescue them. Diana didn't believe a word of it. She was married with a family of her own, and it was far from the first time that her younger sisters had tried to move in with her and her husband. Diana didn't think that her marriage would survive their presence. She was already on the verge of a messy divorce when she got the letter and was faced with a prospect not dissimilar to the one that had faced Gertrude Baniszewski. Becoming a nineteen-year-old single mother was not a tempting prospect, and adding the burden of two more children was too terrifying to contemplate. With the Likens parents' tempestuous relationship, the begging and pleading phone calls from Sylvia and Jenny had become a fairly regular occurrence. Diana disregarded all of Jenny's fairly explicit descriptions of violence and degradation as regular corporal punishment that she was objecting to. She tossed the letter in the trash and went on about her day.

Something about the letter kept on niggling at Diana though. There were details in it, gruesome details, that she wouldn't have expected her little sister to have been capable of fabricating. So eventually she made a shopping trip into Indianapolis and swung by the suburbs on her way into town. One of the children answered the door when she knocked, squinting up at her in the late morning sunshine, but Gert appeared only a moment later. Diana greeted her with a smile. 'Hi there, I heard you're taking care of my sisters? I'm Diana.'

The response that she got just filled her with more apprehension. 'You aren't welcome here.'

'What?'

'Lester. He called me. Said you weren't to see the girls. Said you weren't even to come in the house.'

Diana boggled at her. 'Why on earth would he say something like that?'

'That's family business you've got to sort out between yourselves. But you aren't seeing the girls until I get his say so.' Gert closed the door on her.

All of this was just a little too strange for Diana's liking, so she walked a little further down the street, lit up a cigarette and waited. Almost two hours had passed by the time she got what she was waiting for. Jenny emerged from the house, dragging a sack of garbage almost as big as she was. Diana rushed up to her but instead of the warm welcome she was expecting she got a little yelp of fear. 'I'm not allowed to talk to you. Go away.'

It was all too bizarre. Diana called Indianapolis social services from a payphone and demanded that they investigate before heading home.

A few days later a social worker arrived at the Baniszewski house to find an exasperated Gert waiting for her with a story already prepared. Jenny was present and had been cleaned and dressed up to the best of the Baniszewski girl's abilities. Every word that Gert said, she nodded along with, every insinuation, no matter how vile she agreed with. Gert had cornered her before the social worker arrived and made one thing very clear. If she contradicted Gert in any way, then she was going to be stripped naked and cast down to live in the basement, too. It wasn't any harder to make two little whores disappear than one.

The story that Gert spun the social worker was partly a misdirection and partly the fevered imaginings that she had been inflicting on the Likens girls from the very beginning. Sylvia had been kicked out of the house several weeks ago after Gert discovered that she was physically unclean and a prostitute. Unwilling to expose her own children to Sylvia's lascivious lifestyle, she had decided it was better for them to part ways, but Jenny was silent proof that there was no problem in the house that had driven a teenage girl to turn to prostitution and run away from home. After all, if the good girl was still here, that put all the blame firmly on the bad one. Jenny nodded along. Eyes never once darting over to the door to the basement. She was twitchy and nervous but telling stories about a prostitute in the family was probably stressful enough to cover for her. After the social worker left, Gert gave Jenny a dollar to run to the store and buy herself a treat. After the social worker got back to her office, she closed the case. No more social work calls would be required at the Baniszewski household.

The Freakshow

Gert seemed to have secured her little kingdom for now, but while she had seen to its defences, her children had not been idle. While Gert may have been trapped in a web of her own fantasies, the children lived quite firmly in the real world, and in the real world, their family was on the poverty line. It didn't take long before neighbourhood boys came along who had missed the first 'striptease.' Boys who were eager to see a naked girl for the first time. John started charging boys a nickel to go down into the basement and take a peek. Soon demand began to outstrip supply, so he had to recruit his siblings into the venture. Rather than having their guests trail down into the basement to see her, the emaciated and scarred girl was forced up the stairs to be paraded around on display. She was pawed at, as much as the boys could get away with under the ever-watchful eye of Gert, who somehow still had the obliviousness to launch into searing sermons about the sinfulness of the flesh while having regular sex with a fourteen-year-old boy. Gert wouldn't tolerate Sylvia being used sexually, but violence wasn't just acceptable—it was actively encouraged. Every kid in the neighbourhood had probably taken a swat at the vacant-eyed girl by the end of the first week of displays. A few had stubbed out their cigarettes on her feet. One of the few acts of cruelty that could still draw some sort of response out of her. Sylvia was completely shut down, her motions sluggish and her voice slurring in the brief moments when she had the wherewithal to use it. Burning her drew out a low dull moan. It wasn't enough for the crowd, and the takings from an evening showing of their slave weren't as much as the Baniszewski children hoped to make. So, they started offering a special service. For a quarter, one lucky visitor could be the one to throw Sylvia back down the stairs into the basement.

The only one who was allowed down into the basement without Gert present was Coy Hubbard. She inexplicably trusted the boy, and his loyalty to Stephanie, despite the fact that their relationship had been gradually degenerating ever since the moment he first laid hands on Sylvia. Stephanie had no interest in furthering their physical relationship in defiance of her mother, while Coy got more aggressively sexual every time they were left alone together. Before long their 'relationship' was little more than some perfunctory kissing before he headed down into the basement for the main event. His judo practice with Sylvia lasted even longer now that she was constantly naked, and now that she had no clothes to grapple her with, he was finding new and unexpected hand-holds. He would emerge from the basement drenched in sweat and grinning, then putting Sylvia through her 'hygiene regimen' would be infinitely easier because she'd be too exhausted and sore to fight back.

Days stretched into weeks. Despite all of Gert's best efforts to break her, Sylvia still met the old woman's stares with defiance. It might have seemed to a normal mind that there was nothing more that could be done to the girl. That she had been brought to her lowest point and that the torture had failed. Worse yet, from Gert's perspective, there was no longer any excuse to punish the girl. After all, she wasn't capable of doing anything wrong when she was locked up alone down in the basement. Without sin, there was no reason to cast stones at her. Rationally, Gertrude must have realised that the longer she kept Sylvia down in the basement, the greater the odds that it was going to be discovered. She had total faith in her little army of accomplices, but she knew better than most that the world does not leave you alone just because you keep to yourself. On the 20th of October, they got a reminder of that when a stranger almost made it as far as the basement and the dark secret that they kept locked down there.

The Baniszewski children stole almost constantly with no repercussions from their mother, who could tolerate seeing no fault in her children. So, when a young man named Robert Hanlon showed up on her doorstep demanding the return of his property, she denied all knowledge. The kids had snuck into his basement through an open back door and helped themselves to several items, which were already gracing the shelves of a local pawnshop. Furious, Hanlon waited until nightfall and then broke into the house to try and retrieve his property. He made it as far as the kitchen before he was tackled by Ricky. Coy appeared only a moment later, and between the two of them, the boys were able to drag Hanlon outside and toss him into the street. Gert had called the police to report the intruder and a squad car had arrived shortly afterwards. It was far from the first time that the police had attended the Baniszewski house—Gert had been issued an arrest warrant herself just the year before for failure to pay the paperboy. But it was in all likelihood the first time that Gert had called the police herself, usually preferring to resolve disputes on her own. Hanlon was dragged off to the squad car but the Vermillions unexpectedly interceded on his behalf, explaining the whole situation to the police. It seemed like the police were going to search the house for the stolen goods. It seemed like there was finally some chance that Sylvia was going to be rescued. Then Gert casually asked the officers if any of them knew her husband John. Hanlon was taken down to the station.

After the police cars had all dispersed and quiet had fallen over the house once more, Gert came down to sit with Sylvia in the dark. Her matronly mask plastered back in place. 'I have been thinking about you, Sylvie. You've been in my prayers. I think that the Lord wants me to save you. I think he wants me to give you a second chance at life. Your time down here, that was you doing penance. Turning into something new. Something better than a whore. You want to be more than a toy for men, don't you Sylvie? You want to be free from your sins?'

Sylvia hadn't hoped in a very long time, and even with the ruckus upstairs earlier in the evening, she hadn't really considered the possibility that anything might change. She croaked. 'Yes. I want to be saved.'

'Then I'll help you. But you need to remember. This is your last chance. Your very last chance to do right. Otherwise, it will be back down here before you've even the time to open your filthy mouth. Do you understand?'

Sylvia struggled to wet her lips. 'Yes.'

She was bound hand and foot and carried up the stairs by Gert's boys. They tossed her onto one of the few real beds in the house and Gert crouched down beside her. 'If you can make it through the whole night without pissing yourself, you get to come and live upstairs again with the rest of the humans. Do you think you can do that?'

Sylvia wheezed. 'Yes, mom.'

She could not make it through the night without wetting the bed. While she might have held on to some hope that the very meagre provisions of water that she had drunk the day before would not be sufficient to cause a mess, the damage that had been done when the glass bottle was forced inside her had rendered Sylvia permanently incontinent. Gert came into the room sniffing in the early hours of the morning and then roared with rage, waking the whole house. She came at Sylvia with a knife. The girl looked up at her with helpless terror in her eyes. That one moment was everything that Gert had ever wanted from Sylvia. She used the knife to cut the ropes around Sylvia's wrists, then trailed the knife tip down the length of her body before doing the same with the ligatures around her ankles. She tossed a bundle of dirty clothes at Sylvia and sneered. 'Get yourself dressed whore. I'll not have you parading around in shame all day.'

They made it as far as the living room before Gert's overexcitement had her changing her tune. The boys had migrated through to the living room for their morning smoke, and it didn't take long before Coy and Ricky showed up, like they did most days. The moment she realised there were no girls present, Gert ordered Sylvia to strip. 'Come on, whore.

Give the boys one last show before you go back into the basement.'

Sylvia let out a little sob, but with numb fingers she began to undo the buttons of her borrowed dress, letting it drop to the floor with barely any shame at all. She wore nothing underneath because Gert hadn't given her anything. If the old woman had expected the sight of the naked girl to be exciting to the boys, then she was sorely mistaken. Any hint of sensuality had long since been beaten and starved out of Sylvia. She looked like skin hung over a wire frame. Her eyes locked on some distant horizon that none of the rest of them could see. Gert was furious with her. Even now she was defying her. The whore knew how to put on a show for men and she wasn't even trying. She was so superior. She thought she was better than Gert. She wasn't better than Gert. She wasn't. Snatching up a cola bottle, she slapped it into Sylvia's hand. 'You know what to do, whore. You've done it enough before.'

Sylvia's hand wasn't even shaking as she pushed the glass inside her. Even when she had to grit her teeth to push past the pain, she didn't stop until the bottle was in. She met Gert's stare. Implacable. Then she drew it out just as smoothly and handed it back to the woman. The whore had done exactly what Gert wanted, but it just made her angrier. She snapped. 'Get dressed. You're disgusting.'

Sylvia didn't even try to sit on one of the chairs, gravitating to one of the corners of the room, out of sight and hopefully out of mind. Gert slumped down on a seat in the middle of the room and waited for the rest of the household to filter in. Her plans were coming apart quicker than she could make them. She'd wanted Sylvia to move back upstairs so that she could start punishing her for her misbehaviour again, but instead, the stupid girl had wet herself and now she was going to have to go back into the basement. Then she was meant to be humiliated, putting on a show for the boys, and somehow she'd turned that against Gert, too. She was seething, staring at the girl as she looked off serenely. It was like she wasn't even here. Gert leapt to her feet and pointed a finger at her. 'I didn't forget what you did. You branded my daughters as whores! Now I... Now I shall brand you!'

She ordered the boys forward and they stripped Sylvia out of her clothes again, twisting a sleeve of her dress into a gag and shoving it into her mouth. The children were set to a task. They held one of Gert's sewing needles above a lit match until the metal was glowing orange, then the old woman snatched it out of their hands and advanced on Sylvia with a matching heat in her eyes. The boys pinned Sylvia down and Gert sat on top of her hips. Every one of her ribs was on display and her skin was so pale after a month in the darkness that it was almost translucent. As though she were fading away, unscathed. Gert growled and pressed the needle down into that perfect skin. Dragging a smoking line of pain down the girl's stomach as she thrashed and screamed. Now she was back in the room. Now she was back down here with Gert.

With the letter I completed, Gert reached out for the next needle. All the younger children were set to the task of heating them up, burning through box after box of matches. Gert got as far as 'IM' before she started to tire, and the stinging heat of the needle started to bother her. She handed the next one to Ricky Hobbs and he gleefully took over the punishment. Slowly the words of the brand came into sight. IM A. Ricky paused. 'How do you spell prostitute?'

With a tut, Gert scribbled it onto a piece of paper for him.

Sylvia didn't stop screaming through the whole process and the stench of her burning flesh overpowered even the usual miasma of filth that permeated the house. In the end the words 'IM A PROSTITUTE AND PROUD OF IT' were left engraved into her flesh. Carved out and cauterised in one go. Gert licked her lips and stared gleefully down at the girl she had ruined. 'I'm a prostitute and proud of it. You certainly are, aren't you whore?'

With a contemptuous glance back, Gert left the room to go fetch herself another pack of cigarettes and a new book of matches.

Ricky was still holding on to the needle and without saying anything he passed it back to the ten-year-old Shirley

Baniszewski to heat up again. He hissed. 'Slaves need a brand, so everyone knows that they're owned.'

He gleefully carved the lower half of the letter S into the middle of Sylvia's chest, but at the halfway point he stopped and looked down at what he was doing with growing horror. 'Jenny. Brand your sister.'

Jenny shook her head. He growled. 'Jenny. You do it or so help me...'

She squeaked. 'No. I won't.'

He cast a glance around desperately and then handed the needle to Shirley. 'You finish it. I.. I'm bored.'

Shirley took over the gruesome work with all of the sociopathic joy of a child, but when she was finished scraping the needle across Sylvia's breastbone the letter S had not appeared. Instead, the number 3 was there. Paula cackled at her little sister's stupidity. 'Isn't like you can rub that out and change it!'

Gert came back into the room, puffing away gleefully. She looked at the 3 on Sylvia's chest then chose to ignore it. She tugged the sleeve out of Sylvia's mouth with a cackle. 'What are you going to do now, Sylvie? You can't get married now. You can't undress in front of somebody. No man is going to want you. Nobody is ever going to want you again. What are you going to do now?'

Sylvia drew in a ragged breath but when she answered, it was in her usual voice. All of the fear had been burned away. 'I guess there's nothing I can do. It's on there.'

Even now she was winning. Gert couldn't stand it.

I'm Going to Die

Coy took Sylvia down to the basement and threw her around half-heartedly for a while, but without her terror, it had lost all of its pleasure. He slunk off home for the night, but the usual teenage party picked up in the living room before long. Sylvia lay there in the dark with a cold certainty running through her veins. A terrible, inescapable truth that she whispered when her sister crept down to sit on the stairs in the middle of the night. She whispered, 'I'm going to die. I can tell.'

Jenny tried to comfort her, but her platitudes were short lived. She had to scramble back up to her bed when Gert came around for a visit at about one in the morning.

Gert spent a long time just staring at Sylvia before eventually telling her, 'Come upstairs and go to your bed.'

When Sylvia was struggling, the woman hooked her hands into her armpits and lifted her up, supporting her as she climbed the stairs and then easing her down onto another unspoiled mattress. She gave the girl a pat on the head, then left her to drift off into nightmares that were little worse than her reality.

She slept right through the morning and was only woken gently at midday by Gert and Paula taking her through for a bath. She braced herself for the torture to resume, but the bath was pleasantly warm and full of soapy bubbles. The water stung at her wounds, both the brand and the open sores that had developed in many places over her body, but it was better than it could have been, so she found herself strangely thankful to her tormenters. Afterwards, they helped her get dressed and took her through to the kitchen, where they sat her down at the table with a pen and some paper.

It had been so long since she had dropped out of school in the midst of Gert's early torments that she barely even remembered how to hold the pen. It felt alien in her hand. Still, when the old woman smiled and began to dictate a letter, Sylvia moved to obey her, almost without thinking.

'Dear Mr and Mrs Likens,

I went with a gang of boys in the middle of the night. And they said that they would pay me if I would give them something, so I got in the car and they all got what they wanted... and when they got finished they beat me up and left sores on my face and all over my body. And they also put on my stomach, I am a prostitute and proud of it.

I have done just about everything that I could do just to make Gertie mad and cause Gertie more money than she's got. I've tore up a new mattress and peed on it. I have also cost Gertie doctor bills that she really can't pay and made Gertie a nervous wreck and all her kids.'

Sylvia moved to sign the letter, this obvious fabrication, but Gert snatched it away. 'No. You don't need to sign letters to your own kin. They'll know your writing.'

She turned away and Sylvia was forgotten again. She drifted in a daze for several minutes. Just enjoying the feeling of warmth again after so long in the cold and the dark. She was so disconnected from what was going on around her that she didn't even realise she was being discussed until it was almost over. Gert had her plan all laid out. With this letter as evidence that Sylvia was a runaway, all that remained to be done was to dump her somewhere. It was clear just from looking at her that there wasn't much life left in her. Gert told Paula her intentions. John Junior and Jenny would be told to carry Sylvia to the local garbage dump and leave her there. Exposure would kill her overnight. Once she was out of the house, Gert would go and call the police, and hand them the letter, explaining that Sylvia had gone off with some boys. It isn't clear whether it was due to Gert's mental breakdown or garden variety stupidity that she couldn't understand the flaw in her constructed timeline, but it is likely that the police might have gone along with it due to the renewed presence of John Baniszewski Senior in her life.

Regardless, Sylvia had heard enough. She got to her feet and ran for the front door, as fast as her withered and exhausted legs would carry her. She made it as far as the hallway before Gert scooped her up in her arms and dragged her back into the kitchen, pressing her back into the seat. 'How about some dinner, Sylvie?'

She made toast on the grill and laid it on the table in front of Sylvia with a flourish. Even the blackened, half-stale bread was better fare than she'd experienced in the last month, so Sylvia gobbled it up greedily. Or at least she tried to. Her throat was so swollen from her repeated chokings and the widespread infection that riddled her body that she couldn't force the bread down. She let out a dry sob. 'I can't swallow it.'

Gert's lips thinned. 'Let me help you with that, Sylvie.'

She walked over to the window and Sylvia assumed that she was fetching a glass of water until she heard the fabric tearing.

Gert rushed over with the greasy curtain rod in her hands. Grabbing Sylvia by the hair she tried to ram the end into Sylvia's mouth. Thrusting it in past the girl's cracked lips with a cackle. When Sylvia closed her mouth against the intrusion, Gert started smashing the pole against her teeth instead, eyes wild with some dark lust. 'Take it! Take it, you whore!'

Sylvia toppled onto the floor and Gert spat on her. John Junior arrived to see what all the noise was about and she snapped at him. 'Take the bitch back to her kennel.'

An hour later, Gert had regained her composure. She brought a plate of crackers down and tried to feed them to Sylvia, but the girl just turned her bloodied mouth away. 'Give it to a dog. They're hungrier than I am.'

Gert saw red again. She drove her fist into Sylvia's stomach, over and over until the scabs on her stomach cracked open and blood stained the pretty floral pattern stretched over her desecrated flesh. Gert stormed out of the basement, flicking off the light with a snarl and leaving Sylvia to one last night of total darkness.

On the next day, Gert and Coy came down into the basement together. Sylvia was still lying on the ground in the spot where she had been left. Gert had brought down a chair from the kitchen. She rushed over and swung it at the girl, but misjudged her distance and instead overbalanced and smashed it against the wall. Then she snatched up a paddle and tried to hit Sylvia in the head, but her swing went so wild that she hit herself in the face, blackening her eye. Coy watched, mesmerised by this feat of stupidity, before pushing her aside and hefting the curtain rail in his hands. He beat Sylvia all over her body with the stick, the rhythmic rise and fall of it punctuated only by the wet sounds of its impact.

When they were certain she was unconscious, they abandoned her again.

Sylvia woke in agony in the middle of the night. She tried to scream for help but her throat was too badly damaged to make a sound. She managed to drag herself to the wall, where she found an old spade head, and for hours she beat it against the wall and the floor. Desperately trying to draw attention to her plight. She used every last bit of her strength, hammering away all night long. The noise woke several of the neighbours, but none of them thought to call the police. They were all used to strange noises from the Baniszewski house by now.

The next morning Gert sent Stephanie and Ricky down into the basement to fetch Sylvia for another bath before they disposed of her. They carried her up to the bathroom without even the slightest sign of a struggle and dumped her, fully clothed, into the water. When her face slipped under the water and no bubbles came up, Stephanie realised that something was wrong. They pulled her out of the water and Stephanie tried to perform CPR but it was no use. The body was already cold.

Get Me Out

Jenny sat in the bathroom with her dead sister, staring at her intently and wondering, somewhat treacherously, how long it was going to be until she ended up in the basement now that it had been vacated. Panic swept through the Baniszewski house, but Gert was as solid in her delusions as always. Her plan was going to work just fine. The only thing that needed changed were a couple of minor details. She sent the boys to strip Sylvia and dump her back in the basement until nightfall when they would take her to the dump. Gert herself wandered across the street to call the police from a public phonebooth.

There was an unmistakable tension in the air when the two officers arrived, but Gert pressed on as if everything were fine. She handed them the note that she had forced Sylvia to write, then started waxing lyrical about how much of a burden the young runaway was, and about how inevitable it was that someone who prostituted themselves would end up coming to a gruesome end. The officers read the letter but seemed more perplexed by it than anything else. Even so, this was the wife of a fellow officer and they weren't about to start flinging any accusations around. They took a statement from Gert, and they were heading out of the door before one of them heard Jenny whispering. 'If you get me out of here, I'll tell you everything.'

That was enough to give him pause. He glanced at his partner, who didn't seem to have heard anything.

'I'm going to have to question everyone here. Standard procedure for missing persons.' The tension in the room suddenly mounted. He nodded to Jenny. 'You first, miss.'

The first words out of her mouth once they were out of Gert's line of sight were, 'Look in the basement. They killed her.'

He left Jenny in that strange bedroom with no door and went to his partner to ensure nobody left the building. Then he went down the staircase into hell.

Everyone in the house was arrested. Gert, Paula, Stephanie, John Junior, Coy, and Ricky were all arrested on murder charges. Everyone else was arrested for assault and injury to a person. Officers flitted out through the city, serving arrest warrants to everyone else involved in the horrific story and outside of Coy, Ricky and the Baniszewskis, every single one of them immediately told the police everything that they knew. From neighbourhood children to the local reverend. Everything came out, and all of it ended up in the court documents.

An autopsy was carried out on Sylvia's body to see which story was corroborated by the evidence. Gert's deranged tale of pregnant teenage prostitutes and roaming bands of torture hungry boys, or Jenny's even more disturbing story of matriarchal torment. Over one hundred cigarette burns were found on Sylvia's body. She had suffered second and third-degree burns. There was severe bruising, muscular and nerve damage. The cause of death seemed to have been multiple brain haemorrhages, but it was just as possible that the combined shock of all her injuries had just been too much for her weakened body to tolerate. In her death throes, Sylvia had bitten through her own lips, leaving them attached only by trailing threads of connective tissue. Her throat and vagina had swollen shut, although an examination of the canal revealed that her hymen was intact. Combined with the lack of rectal scar tissue, this made the obvious falsity of Gert's stories apparent to everyone involved.

The Trials of Gertrude Baniszewski

All of the lesser charges were ultimately dropped thanks to all the evidence that had been provided, with only the murder charge being upheld against Gert, her daughters, John Junior, Coy, and Ricky. When the case went to trial, the maelstrom of chaos that characterised their lives followed along with them. The charges against Stephanie were dropped before the case went to trial after she turned state's witness against her family—furnishing us with most of the story that we now know about the bizarre events within the Baniszewski home while downplaying her own culpability at every turn. Each of the plaintiffs had their own lawyer, with the exception of John and Coy, who were both underage and trying to pursue their youth as a defence. It had become apparent very early on that everyone involved was guilty to one degree or another, and only the degree of blame that would be individually assigned would determine which of them died and which of them escaped lethal injection.

Paula was rushed out of the courtroom during her first appearance to give birth to her daughter, whom she named Gertrude, after her mother, and from then the circus only grew more ludicrous. While the children all cottoned on to John and Coy's tactic early on, claiming that they were merely coerced accomplices to Gert's madness, the woman herself seemed to be pursuing a completely different line of defence from her lawyer. The lawyer argued that Gert was old, infirm, and mentally impaired and that the children had done whatever they pleased in the absence of competent supervision in a sort of 'Lord of the Flies' scenario.

If anything, this argument was supported by Gert's own ridiculous behaviour throughout the trial, but after a certain point she began damning herself with her own testimony. She loudly announced to the court that Sylvia Likens had been the neighbourhood whore. Then she fabricated longwinded stories about the girl's trysts with married men, insisted vehemently on the girl's pregnancy and regaled the court with tales of all the times that she had started fights in her household, like some cuckoo hatchling snuck into the nest, intent on killing all the other chicks. She had no evidence to support her claims, and indeed it went completely against what much of the physical evidence gathered told the court, but she did have one witness willing to back up every single story that she told: her eleven-year-old daughter Marie. During her own testimony, Marie repeated everything that Gert had said, mostly verbatim, but during cross-examination she quickly broke down, screaming 'God help me!' before admitting that everything she and her mother had said up until that point was a lie. Her testimony, describing in blunt detail how her mother and siblings had tortured and ultimately murdered Sylvia Likens, was considered to be the turning point in the case. Gert was found guilty of murder in the first degree. To the dismay of the public, she was granted a sentence of life imprisonment without the possibility of parole instead of the death penalty.

Paula was convicted of second-degree murder. She appealed and was granted a second trial, but before she came to court she made a plea bargain, admitting to voluntary manslaughter. She served three years on that charge before she was paroled and then moved to a life of obscurity in Iowa at least until 2012 when she was exposed on Facebook and lost her job as a teacher's aide, in which she had been taking care of other people's children for years with nobody any the wiser.

John, Coy, and Ricky were all convicted of voluntary manslaughter and condemned to eighteen months in a juvenile detention facility.

John served his sentence, admitted full culpability to his crimes in interviews and seemed to be the only member of the family to experience true remorse. He went on to live a halfway-to-decent life, heavily involved with the church until complications from his diabetes resulted in his death in 2005.

Coy showed absolutely no remorse for his crimes and based on the evidence it is likely due to his being both a sexual sadist and a psychopath, just waiting for an opportunity to arise. He remained a criminal following his time in prison and was later charged with another double murder after a home invasion robbery went awry. While he tried to stay out of the limelight, attention to the Likens case has resulted in him being identified and losing several jobs over the years.

Ricky came out of the juvenile detention facility a changed man, but not for the better. He recognised his own culpability in Sylvia's murder and suffered a nervous breakdown shortly after his release. He lost a great deal of weight while imprisoned, and it was only after he had finally started to regain his faculties following his breakdown that he was finally diagnosed with late stage lung cancer. He died soon afterwards, riddled with tumours and regrets.

Gertrude Baniszewski appealed against her conviction on the basis of the extremely prejudicial atmosphere in Indianapolis, and the fact that the judge had been unwilling to let the case be relocated was considered to be solid enough proof of a mistrial, so her appeal for a retrial was granted.

Without the damning testimony of her own preteen daughter, the jury was more lenient on Gert this time around. She was condemned to only eighteen years in prison.

She made herself into a model prisoner during her time inside, becoming a mother figure to many of the other inmates and working in the sewing shop. By the time that she came up for parole in 1985, she was widely referred to as 'Mom' by both the inmates and the guards.

Jenny Likens was adopted into the family of the prosecutor from the original case, Leroy New. He had several daughters of his own and she was well liked. She did her best to forget what had happened to her sister, but when news of Gert's parole hearing reached her, she felt obliged to take action. She made television appearances alongside many victims' rights advocates, condemning Indianapolis for even considering releasing the unrepentant monster. Even during her parole hearing, Gert still wouldn't admit to any wrongdoing. After a petition with forty thousand signatures was delivered to the parole board she was heard to exclaim, 'I'm not sure what role I had in it because I was on drugs. I never really knew her. I take full responsibility for whatever happened to Sylvia. I wish I could undo it but I can't and I'm sorry. I'm just asking for mercy and nothing else.'

After her parole was granted, Gert changed her name to Nadine Van Fossan and went to live with her daughter Paula. She was secretive during those years, with good reason. There was a whole, furious world out there that would have happily wrought revenge upon her for the death of Sylvia. She survived for only five years outside of captivity before succumbing to lung cancer in 1990.

It is quite possible that we will never know the truth about what happened to Sylvia Likens. Her story has now been shared in books and films, but every one of them has been based on testimony from the various members of the Baniszewski family, rooted entirely in their self-defensive lies. There have been many theories about what drove Gert to torture a young woman in the prime of her life to death, and indeed many of her Freudian slips throughout her ranting and raving seem to indicate that she saw herself in Sylvia. A version of herself that had not fallen so far from grace. One that could perhaps be kept right with strong enough discipline. Either that or Sylvia was simply serving as a punching bag for a woman so full of self-loathing that it overflowed and destroyed not only her own family but an innocent girl, too.

It is clear that Gert suffered from some sort of mental impairment which informed her actions, and it is entirely plausible that drugs or mental illness were clouding her judgement, but the death of Sylvia Likens was not a crime of passion. It did not happen in a moment of madness. The slow progressive torture that led to that girl's death went on for months. Even if we accept that Gert was somehow oblivious to the evil of her actions, that does not explain why the rest of the vast safety net of society completely failed the girl too.

There was an entire neighbourhood aware of the situation in the Baniszewski house, if not in full, then certainly in part. Yet not one of them contacted the police when they saw a girl shed half her body weight, wander the streets with open sores or black eyes. Not one person who crossed Sylvia Likens' path stopped and put in the bare minimum of effort that could have prevented her untimely demise.

There is no bottom to the pit of blame surrounding the death of Sylvia Likens. But you can be certain that at least some portion of it must be laid at the feet of the matriarch of the Baniszewski clan, whose delusions seemed to be so powerful that they could carry a dozen teenagers along for the ride and that could transform an unfortunate girl into the victim of what has been described as the single worst crime perpetrated against an individual in all of human history.

About the Author

Ryan Green is a true crime author in his late thirties. He lives in Herefordshire, England with his wife, three children, and two dogs. Outside of writing and spending time with his family, Ryan enjoys walking, reading and windsurfing.

Ryan is fascinated with History, Psychology and True Crime. In 2015, he finally started researching and writing his own work and at the end of the year, he released his first book on Britain's most notorious serial killer, Harold Shipman.

He has since written several books on lesser-known subjects, and taken the unique approach of writing from the killer's perspective. He narrates some of the most chilling scenes you'll encounter in the True Crime genre.

You can sign up to Ryan's newsletter to receive a free book, updates, and the latest releases at:

WWW.RYANGREENBOOKS.COM

Other Titles by Ryan Green

If you enjoyed reading *Torture Mom* you may like these other titles by Ryan Green:

Harold Shipman: The True Story of Britain's Most Notorious Serial Killer

Colombian Killers: The True Stories of the Three Most Prolific Serial Killers on Earth

Fred & Rose West: Britain's Most Infamous Killer Couples

The Kuřim Case: A Terrifying True Story of Child Abuse, Cults & Cannibalism

Obeying Evil: The Mockingbird Hill Massacre Through the Eyes of a Killer

The Truro Murders: The Sex Killing Spree Through the Eyes of an Accomplice

Sinclair: The World's End Murders through the Eyes of a Killer

You Think You Know Me: The True Story of Herb Baumeister and the Horror at Fox Hollow Farm

Made in the USA
Las Vegas, NV
05 August 2021